Healing Violent Men

DATE DUE

DATE DUE

FEB 1 0 2004	

DEMCO, INC. 38-2931

Healing Violent Men

A Model for Christian Communities

David J. Livingston

Fortress Press

MINNEAPOLIS

HEALING VIOLENT MEN
A Model for Christian Communities

Cover art: *Migrating Birds* by Ayako Araki. Used by permission of the Asian Christian Art Association, Yogyakarta, Indonesia.
Cover design: Marti Naughton
Interior design: Peregrine Graphics Services

The poem at the beginning of chapter 3, "Balloon Heart," is from *Bodies That Hum* by Beth Gylys and is used by permission of Silverfish Review Press.
The poem at the beginning of chapter 5, "Setting Out," is from *The Wheel* by Wendell Berry. Copyright © 1982 by Wendell Berry. Reprinted by permission of North Point Press, a division of Farrar, Straus and Giroux, LLC.
Appendices 1 and 2, "Indicators That a Man May Kill His Partner" and "Accountability," are taken from the publication *Accountability: Program Standards for Batterer Intervention* by Barbara Hart and are used by permission of the Pennsylvania Coalition against Domestic Violence.
Figure 2 in chapter 1, "The Power and Control Wheel," and Figure 5 in chapter 3, "The Equality Wheel," are reprinted with permission of the Domestic Abuse Intervention Project, 202 E. Superior St., Duluth, Minnesota 55802.
Scripture texts used in this work are taken from the *New American Bible,* copyright © 1970 by the Confraternity of Christian Doctrine, Washington, D.C., and are used by permission of the copyright owner. All rights reserved.

ISBN 0-8006-3251-6

The paper used in this publication meets the minimum requirements of American National Standard for Information Sciences—Permanence of Paper for Printed Library Materials, ANSI Z329.48-1984.

Manufactured in the U.S.A.   AF 1-3251
06   05   04   03   02   1   2   3   4   5   6   7   8   9   10

Contents

TO
Joan, Matt, and Sara

Preface

This project arises as a theological response to working with men who have been violent with their wives, lovers, and children. Having spent several years challenging the beliefs and confronting the denial of violent offenders, I have heard men tell their stories and have seen their victims' bruises, as well as their children's anguished and often futile attempts to "understand" the violence between their parents.[1] The broken lives and bodies of these women and children, along with the confusion, arrogance, and despair of these men, are the concrete foundation to which this project will return as its final referent and judge.

Before I can discuss even the methodological concerns of the project as a whole, I must address the political character of this work. This project is not an attempt to universalize and demonize men. I am attempting to address intimate relationships as they present themselves in the diversity of the North American culture. I have confined my reflections to relationships that have opposite-gender partners, although I am well aware of the amount of pain and suffering also endured daily within the gay and lesbian communities because of intimate violence. I believe some of the reflections below will resonate with the experience of single-gender relationships, but I am not venturing to examine these relationships in their uniqueness.

I have further confined my reflections to the preponderance of literature in the field, which supports the proposal that men, even if they are no more likely to strike their partner than are women, are far more likely to inflict harm and to intimidate their partner. I have also focused on male violence toward women within intimate relationships because I have worked with these men. I believe that it is my role as a white male theologian to reflect on the potential for violation and reconciliation. I assume a decidedly pro-feminist orientation, which I believe is also pro-male, when I attempt to understand and ameliorate, if not eliminate, the violence that occurs through the hands of men on the people they claim to love.

In other words, in this work I do not specifically address two distracting and unhelpful lines of thought: the question of women's violence toward men, and the reality that most men are not violent toward their partners. I want to discuss the gendered character of violence without constantly footnoting and apologizing in reference to literature that would argue that my claims are essentialist from the start. I believe, and I will attempt to show in chapters 1 and 2, that the power dynamics of male-female intimate relationships tend to have a certain sedimented character that, when lived out, has potential to reinforce the violence as well as mock authentic reconciliation. This in no way minimizes or denies the potential of women to do violence toward their partners and their children. Nor does it imply a simplification of the nuanced reflections on gender that continue to enhance our understanding of who we are. I wish only to claim that men have a potential within relationships to engage in violent behavior. This potential reflects their sense of gendered identity, endures over time, and requires an ecclesial response that moves beyond demonization or denial of responsibility.

The first step of the analysis is to engage the phenomenon of intimate violence itself in all its complexity and diversity and to attempt, through a careful examination, to pull out of this phenomenon certain modes of relationality that are violated. For this reason, the analysis in the first chapters progresses from an extended reflection on the phenomenon of violence itself and specifically of intimate violence (chapter 1), through a reflection on the nature of violence and its cultural underpinnings (chapter 2), followed by a sociocultural analysis of the symbols of marriage, and reconciliation and the impact these symbols have on the lived experience of both perpetrator and survivor (chapter 3).

The second portion of the project occurs in two chapters that draw upon this phenomenology to reconstruct the doctrine of reconciliation in terms of "re-conciliation," that is, a re-admission to the ecclesial community. Reconciliation focuses on a sense of primary relationality that is grounded in responsibility, rather than a desire for reunion of those separated by the violence. Chapter 4 proposes that reconciliation may be understood as a deep symbol of the tradition. It holds in tension a call for unending responsibility and therefore a refusal of simple reunion, on the one hand, and a Christian demand for forgiveness and love that requires all to be reconciled to the ecclesial body, even if not to the violated partner, on the other. The book concludes with the application of the conclusions of chapter 4 into practical approaches to serving violent men in both the parish community and the larger society.

I wish to thank several people who have helped me through this daunting task. First, I wish to thank Joan, my friend, my partner, and my lifelong companion, who has been so supportive and encouraging over the past ten years. Without her help, this project would never have been completed. I also wish to thank Matt and Sara for their laughter and joy, which always gave me perspective when I was lost within the doubt that accompanies writing. My parents have been so supportive of me throughout this whole process in so many ways; it is certain that without them this project would never have been completed. Friends are an invaluable gift. Jack, Barb, Sus, Mark, Laurel, Donna, Scott, Mike, Chris, Sarah, Pam, Steve, Dennis, Tom, Mary, Dorothy, Therese, Alice, Ralph, Beth, Michelle, and Gerry have been friends in the deepest sense of the term; they have often corrected my path, both intellectually and spiritually, and they have always been willing to listen. My colleagues at Mercyhurst College have been willing to listen to my ideas and debate some of the finer points of the argument. The administration at Mercyhurst, especially William Garvey, Andrew Roth, and Joseph Gower, has been very supportive of my research. I wish to thank all the other friends who are too numerous to mention, but who, together, have provided an encouraging voice for me during this often lonely process. Finally, I wish to thank the readers of earlier versions of this work: Edward Farley, Susan Brooks Thistlethwaite, Jim Poling, Howard Harrod, Peter Hodgson,

Liston Mills, Paul Dokecki, and Sallie McFague, who have been supportive and encouraging throughout the process. I wish especially to thank Edward Farley for his generosity and critical support over the last eight years. He is and will always be an inspiration to my work.

1

Violent Men in Our Communities: The Dynamics of Intimate Violence

My heart pounds within me;
  death's terrors fall upon me.
If an enemy had reviled me,
  that I could bear.
If my foe had viewed me with contempt,
  from that I could hide.
But it was you, my other self,
  my comrade and friend,
You, whose company I enjoyed
  at whose side I walked in procession . . .
Softer than butter is [your] speech,
  but war is in [your] heart.
Smoother than oil are [your] words,
  but [you] are an unsheathed sword.

PSALM 55

Intimate violence strikes at the very heart of the love relationship. The psalmist understood this. He knew that the most painful experience is not the violation one experiences at the hands of one's enemies. Instead, it is the violation that occurs within the context of intimacy that is virtually unbearable. This violence is "death's terror." For we come to relationships with expectations. The expectations of those who fall in love do not include abuse, scorn, manipulation, or assault. When love is coupled with violence, our neat categories break down and we fail in our attempts to make sense of our world. This first chapter will make an initial step in this difficult process of understanding how intimacy and violence can exist in the same relationship. The chapter will uncover the dynamics of intimate violence as a means of providing

1

an essential understanding, which is a prerequisite to the goal of holding men responsible while also offering healing and hope.

The Christian community has not responded well to the paradox of domestic violence. The categories of "intimate violence" and "marital rape" create what classical Greek philosophy terms an *aporia* and what we often term a paradox. How can two terms so diametrically opposed be held together? It would be bearable if intimate violence were just another philosophical conundrum, but it is the lived experience of hundreds of thousands of women and children. They do not have the luxury of putting down the book and shaking their head when it becomes too confusing. They live in an absurd world where love means pain and commitment means isolation and imprisonment.

Recent years have witnessed some strides toward protecting women and children who suffer from violence in the home. Though these movements are encouraging, they are inadequate. Even more discouraging is the absence of conversation and action regarding the source of the abuse: violent men. The Christian community must take on the responsibility of healing the broken and calling the perpetrators to conversion. To answer this call, we must have a clear understanding of the dynamics of domestic violence and the process of healing and conversion. This book explores the deep well of healing available to perpetrators and survivors within the Christian tradition and offers a hopeful vision of relationships without violence.

Pastors, therapists, and social workers meet men every day who act as if women are inferior and should function as servants and obedient wives, lovers, and mothers. It is clear that these men are becoming less and less common, but among them is a percentage whose expectations are not met. These men resort to violence in order to force their partners to conform to their vision of the way the world should be. Men who feel comfortable only when they are in control of the world around them do not function well within relationships, because relationships involve another person who has goals, dreams, and ideas of her or his own. When a lover becomes an intimidating, violent assailant, society and the church often want to turn away and claim that it is a private matter. As personal and private as erotic loving relationships may be, when they become permeated with anger, intimidation, and violence, the community must offer protection and support. If the church community does not care for the vulnerable and abused within its own circle, it becomes an ineffectual voice for justice in the larger community.

The Ambiguity of Reconciliation

To discuss the phenomenon of intimate violence, its perpetrators and survivors, and the dynamics involved between these agents, we must first understand how such things are humanly possible. We must also see these dynamics within a larger framework that includes the appropriateness of reconciliation. As I argue below, the human is a relational being who has the capacity to violate and be violated, as well as the capacity to heal and to forgive, and must be open to transformation through a critical praxis. It must also be possible to draw from the many individual experiences and unique relationships some abstractions or theoretical reflections that combine to provide a relatively adequate description of the dynamics present in intimate violence. I maintain that the symbols present in the Judeo-Christian tradition, in spite of their capacity for ongoing dehumanization, also contain resources that can call us beyond violation and toward the formation of increasingly nurturing relationships.

In his book *The Analogical Imagination,* David Tracy introduces the idea of the classic. Classics are disclosive and transformative symbols that persevere from generation to generation and have the capacity to carry the wisdom as well as the distortions of the status quo of a previous epoch. Tracy states:

> My thesis is that what we mean in naming certain texts, events, images, rituals, symbols and persons "classics" is that here we recognize nothing less than the disclosure of a reality we cannot but name truth. . . . Here we find something valuable, something "important"; some disclosure of reality in a moment that must be

called one of "recognition" which surprises, provokes, challenges, shocks and eventually transforms us; an experience that upsets conventional opinion and expands the sense of the possible; indeed a realized experience of that which is essential, that which endures.[1]

Many classic symbols exist within the Christian tradition, including sin, hope, heaven, messiah, and grace. The classic that we will be examining throughout this project is that of "reconciliation." Reconciliation is a fundamental symbol of the Christian tradition. Reconciliation is distinct from forgiveness because it involves more than forgiveness and is a communal rather than an individual phenomenon. Reconciliation has its linguistic roots in *re-conciliation,* that is, rejoining the *concilium* or community.[2] This aspect of rejoining the community is distinct from reunion, which is merely re-uniting something that was once a unity or a single entity. Instead we speak of rejoining a community, a community where each member has his or her own autonomy but also needs the support of the others in the community. The question we are asking is whether a violation within the community calls for reconciliation or ostracism.

According to David Tracy, one must enter into a symbol as one enters a game: the first step must be complete immersion into the symbol, and only then can one begin the necessary task of reflection and criticism.[3] If one delves deeply into the symbol of reconciliation, one is forced to accept that it is possible to find a place for even the most violent of people within the confines of the ecclesial community.[4] I am not referring to the Roman Catholic sacrament of reconciliation. Rather, I am referring to a deep symbol[5] that is rooted in the sacramental tradition of Christianity but is also present in the lived experience of Christian men and women as they confront the brokenness of daily life. A description of the full context and meaning of the symbol of reconciliation based in responsibility is not possible at this point, but an example of how one enters into reconciliation before one critically examines all the theories is present in the 1995 movie *Dead Man Walking.*[6]

Encountering Violent Men:
Revulsion and Hope

In *Dead Man Walking*, a brutal rape and murder scene is slowly unveiled alongside the relationship of Sr. Helen Prejean and Pat Sonnier. The dramatization of Sonnier raping a young woman and murdering the young man who was with her stands as a conspicuous cultural manifestation of the phenomenon I hope to address. Is "reconciliation" possible or even desirable for those who commit such acts of brutality? In the film, the fundamental repulsion for violence and for the violator, the desire for revenge, and the opposition to forgiveness are all present. There arises especially intense anger and frustration with Sr. Helen's attempts at reconciliation. What does it mean to talk about reconciliation for Pat Sonnier or for the many other men who abuse, beat, rape, torture, or kill their partners? Is reconciliation possible, or just?

In the film, Sr. Helen is asked by a friend to be a spiritual advisor to a person on death row. She agrees before she is fully aware of Sonnier's crime. She meets with Pat and treats him as a human before and while she is also forming a mental picture of the crime and the suffering of the victims. She is engaged in the process of reconciliation before she can become critical of her relationship with Pat Sonnier. After she has come to see that he is human (and this acknowledgment is the first step of the process of reconciliation), she then questions whether she should be involved in "helping" him.

This sequence tracks well with Tracy's insistence on the need to engage the classic symbol of reconciliation before we dismiss the possibility of its power. Tracy's method is meant to take seriously the evil present in our lived experiences. He notes the perennial ambiguity of human circumstance, the presence of evil and good we find mixed into our communal existence. For Tracy, ambiguity is the tensive character of history itself, the tension of "great good and frightening evil" existing in the same event. Certainly, the symbol of reconciliation has an ambiguous history, one wrought with death and torture for the sake of "unity." Evil and good exist as "both/and" rather than "either/or" in history. Relationships in which intimate violence exists are both intimate and violent. It is far easier to state that the woman is "stupid for staying with him" than it is to address the complexity of the "both/and" character of intimate violence.

Tracy presents a basic motif of responsibility as an initial means of acting in light of history's interruptions. He borrows from Abraham Joshua Heschel, who insists, "Not all are guilty, but all are responsible."[7] Here, responsibility is understood in the sense of being capable of responding. Responsibility begins with the step of accepting ambiguity, of accepting the complex dialectic of good and evil in history. It involves resisting any history that accepts only the good.

The classical Christian symbolism I juxtapose to the experience of intimate violence is the tradition's claim of the possibility of reconciliation. That is, can the classic proclaim that reconciliation is actually possible in history? Can the classic maintain that violence will not have the final word? If the answer to both of these questions is yes, and I believe it is, then the classic symbol of reconciliation, in spite of its ambiguity, remains a living one. We should not be misled into thinking that the churches have some magic that will "cure" all men of any desire for power and control. My personal experience has been that most men convicted of battering their partners return to behaviors that further violate their partners and children. Faced with this experience and the preponderance of evidence in the social-scientific research, I argue against the possibility of "perfect" rehabilitation. At the same time, I maintain hope that reconciliation based on a re-entrance into a community not only is possible but is the demand of the Christian call for reconciliation.

Working with Violent Men

When I began working with violent men in 1991, I was naïve. I quickly became disillusioned and jaded. Working with violent men made me question myself. Was I helping to encourage the long-term abuse and neglect of women and children through attempting to "counsel" these men? Many men appear to use what they learn in group settings to abuse their partner further. By offering men examples of how other men intimidate, control, and isolate their partner, was I offering the batterer in treatment a new arsenal of techniques and ideas? I could see some progress in the men I worked with, but I remained completely certain that I would fear for her safety if my daughter chose to date any of the men in the group. Yet I also discovered a place beyond this state of disillusionment, a way of being in the world that recognizes the need for responsibility and consistent wariness but also believes in hope. Paul Ricoeur has talked about this latter stage as a second naïveté, a state I have come to in relation to the dynamics of domestic violence. It is not a return to the initial naïve approach but a hopeful and passionate perspective that has been challenged and tested. Domestic violence is one of the most difficult human phenomena that we as a church community attempt to address. It seems absurd that a relationship that is supposed to be based on love can become violent and demeaning. The incredulity is stretched even further when the relationship does not dissolve but instead continues in a cycle of apparent forgiveness and sentimental love followed by increased violence.

The Dynamics of Domestic Violence

The dynamics of domestic violence must be clearly understood by pastoral professionals working with couples in various contexts. Further, it is the responsibility of the church community to advocate for those who suffer abuse at the hands of their partners. Advocacy for the safety and well-being of those violated is an important concern of this work, though not the central one. Many excellent books offer pastoral guidance on the church's relationship to survivors of domestic violence, and many of them can be found in this book's bibliography. I believe that these books have done an excellent job of addressing the needs of abused women, but the batterers are most often discussed only in relation to the women and children they have abused. Here I focus my reflections on the men who are abusive and the relationship that the church should have to these men. This book addresses the cause of the violence and claims that through a responsible, loving response to the batterer, the church community fulfills its call to "Love your enemies, and pray for those who persecute you" (Matt. 5:44). This is not a simple love but a complex dynamic of disciplined watchfulness and patient encouragement. Men who have been violent with their partners are members of our towns and cities and also members of our church communities. Our communities cannot abandon these men; abandonment will only exacerbate their situation. The Christian community has already done enough to endorse this violent behavior, as we will see in chapter 3, but to neglect the responsibility to love and serve even the most violent and often unlikable people is unacceptable.

How does domestic violence occur, and what are its recurring characteristics? I draw on my own personal experience working with batterers as well as the social-scientific research of the last two decades to outline the basic features and to move from understanding to structural change. It is only after one comes to understand how men choose to be violent and why there remains a sense of desire to stay together after the violence that one can move on to an appropriate response to intimate violence. I begin this analysis with a portrayal of a violent man. His story is not unique; in fact, its banality is what is most disturbing.

James's Story

James,[8] a member of a batterers' treatment group, had been consistently denying any responsibility for his being sentenced to mandatory treatment in a batterers' program. His file indicated that his partner, after the most recent assault, had been in an emergency room with a broken arm. In spite of the seemingly clear physical evidence, James refused to claim any responsibility for about three months. His story at group check-in, a time when each man tells the reason for his being ordered by a court into the group, became increasingly inconsistent. Finally, during his fourth month, James began check-in almost timidly, saying he had been mowing the lawn before he and his partner were to leave for a family picnic:

> I came in from outside, and she was on the phone with her sister. I gave her "a look," then went in and took a shower, but when I came out she was still on the phone. I just walked over and calmly hung up the phone, saying it was time to go. We started arguing, and the argument turned into a shouting match. I grabbed her and threw her on the floor. When she got up, I grabbed her by the hair and threw her into the wall, and then threw her on the floor again.

During this beating, his partner's arm was broken, and she received a concussion.

James's willingness to tell this story to the group signaled progress; he seemed to be moving through his denial and toward some level of accountability. James continued to work in the program for the next two months, and his accountability continued to improve. He began living with his partner again. James finished the program and appeared to have taken some insights with him. Four months later, while I was working in court, I saw James's name on the docket; he was charged with assault. When I talked with him, I asked him what had happened. He did not deny hitting his partner but blamed her for his "need" to hit her. James relayed the incident to me as follows:

> I told her to call the repairman about fixing the air conditioner. When I came home from work, the house felt like it was 120 degrees inside. She was gone, and there was a note saying she had gone to the mall and then would pick up our son from baseball practice. As I sat in the heat, I was getting more and more angry. My wife and son arrived home about 8:00. She said she had decided to go out to dinner since it was so hot at home. I couldn't believe I had been sitting home in the heat, and she had been spending my money on dinner in an air-conditioned restaurant. I asked her about the repair of the air conditioner, and she gave me some smart answer, so I just backhanded her.

I saw his partner that afternoon, and her face was badly bruised. The bruises on her face appeared to have arisen from much more than a "backhand."

Banal in its details, the above account presents the phenomenon of intimate violence without glamorizing or minimizing it. It is representative of the "normalcy" that intimate violence takes on in many homes. James's simple accounting of his story creates the illusion of its being a minor incident. The fear and violation caused by these "minor incidents" are the focal point of this chapter.

Stories of brutal and ongoing crimes involving very vicious acts on the part of men are common. I do not wish to minimize the horror of many women's experiences of marital rape and ongoing beatings, but I wish here to focus attention on the "normalcy" or routine occurrence of intimate violence, which is perpetrated by average men in rural communities, small towns, and large cities every day. If we allow the phenomenon to become an "unthinkable crime," one committed only by "monsters," we demonize the men. By demonizing them, we allow ourselves to avoid the reality of just how common intimate violence is and how often it is hidden from our sight by the privacy of the home. According to the National Violence against Women Survey, 52 percent of women stated that they have been physically assaulted at some time in their life; 1.9 million women are assaulted every year in the United States. The statistics for rape are equally troubling. Eighteen percent of women stated that they had experienced an attempted or completed rape at some time in their life, and of those who reported being raped, 22 percent stated that they were under the age of twelve when they were first raped. Twenty-five percent of the women surveyed reported partner violence compared with 8 percent of the men reporting partner violence.[9] In addition to ignoring the prevalence of the problem, we also allow ourselves to relinquish our responsibility for caring for the men, women, and children involved in intimate violence.

The research of clinicians and the studies of criminology, psychology, and sociology allow us to present the three basic dynamics of intimate violence. The data for these dynamics is drawn from conversations and studies with the men who commit these acts of violence and the women who suffer from them. First, intimate violence has a repetitive or cyclical pattern. Second, the repetitive nature of intimate violence creates a psychosocial dynamic within the relationship, in which the perpetrator and survivor become intensely bonded because of, not in spite of, the violence. Third, stalking and homicide can become serious dangers when the survivor of the violence terminates a violent relationship.

Before I can move any further in my analysis of intimate violence, we must define the parameters of the term. I define intimate violence as *an act that harms, restricts, or violates another person within the context of an erotic or marital relationship.*[10] I use the term *erotic* to denote the partnered intimacy of people, married or not, who may or may not "love" each other, but who live in a relationship that is different in its form of intimacy because, on some level, it does involve or has involved erotic love. Within the context of these erotic intimate relationships, violence occurs, and it is this violence that will be examined. The violations are not just physical, as noted in the following definition by James Poling:

> Domestic violence is a pattern of assaultive and coercive behaviors, including physical, sexual, and psychological attacks, as well as economic coercion, that adults or adolescents use against their intimate partners (including physical assaults, sexual assaults, psychological assaults, threats of violence and harm, attacks against property or pets and other acts of intimidation, emotional abuse, isolation, use of children, and use of economics).[11]

With these definitions, we limit our discussion to the field of research that has often been termed *domestic violence* or *family violence*.

The Cycle of Violence

In 1979, Lenore Walker wrote what was to become a classic text in the field of domestic violence research, *The Battered Woman.* In *The Battered Woman* and its companion volume, *The Battered*

Woman Syndrome, Walker argues that intimate violence occurs as a repetitive cycle of abuse and that the women who suffer from this abuse can develop a debilitating psychosocial coping mechanism termed "Battered Woman Syndrome."[12] According to Walker, there are three stages that make up the cycle of violence: (1) the tension-building phase, (2) the acute battering phase, and (3) the loving contrition phase (see Figure 1).[13]

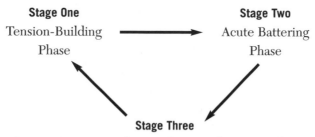

Stage One
Tension-Building
Phase

Stage Two
Acute Battering
Phase

Stage Three
Loving Contrition Phase and Desire for Reconciliation

Figure 1: The Cycle of Violence

The Stages of Violence

Adapting Lenore Walker's theory, we can note the following characteristics of the three stages of violence:

Stage 1: Tension-Building Phase

- Woman can sense man's edginess.
- Little issues are smoothed over.
- Woman feels she can and must control the situation.
- Woman denies her anger.
- Woman feels she deserves it.
- In order to cope, she denies that the second stage will occur and believes she has control.
- Although she is often unaware of it, after each incident her anger grows.

- He knows his behavior is wrong and fears she will leave him.
- She reinforces his fear by withdrawing herself in order not to set him off.
- His jealousy and smothering brutality increase.
- Tension rises.
- Sometimes the woman knows that Stage 2 must come and provokes the attack in order to get it over with and to have it on her terms. She can then feel she has some control.

Stage 2: Acute Battering Phase
- In Stage 1 the man accepts that his rage is out of control but justifies it. In Stage 2, he no longer understands his anger.
- The man doesn't begin by wanting to hurt the woman, but to teach her a lesson or punish her.
- A woman can often retell this stage in detail. The man often claims he cannot.
- Women often feel that it is safe to release their anger and fight back.
- This is the shortest stage and generally lasts from a few hours to forty-eight hours.
- It is unclear why he stops. He seems to know how to prolong the battering without killing her.
- It is not uncommon for a man to wake the woman up and begin to beat her.
- A woman will often deny the seriousness of her injuries, sometimes to soothe the batterer and to be assured that Stage 2 is over.

Stage 3: Loving Contrition Phase
- The stage is welcomed by both.
- The man is sorry and tries to make up.
- He feels she will leave him.
- He is charming and manipulative.
- He believes he can control himself and will never again hurt the woman he loves.
- He convinces everyone.

- The woman wants to believe him and convinces herself.
- She has a glimpse of her original view of how nice love is.
- This is a very idealized stage—little girl loved by husband or lover.
- He plays dependent—he will fall apart without her.
- She ends up feeling responsible for him as well as for her own victimization.
- She is given whatever she wants, with overkill—flowers, candy, presents.
- This stage is generally longer than Stage 2 and shorter than Stage 1.

In Walker's case studies, these stages repeat themselves in a cycle that increases in severity of abuse even while the interval of time involved in each stage decreases. Over time, the cycle begins to move through its three stages so quickly that the first and third stages almost disappear. At this point, it can appear as if the relationship involves nothing but one instance of acute battering followed by another.[14]

Walker's model suggests that a pattern of relation, tension, acute violence, contrition, and reunion exists in most relationships of intimate violence. A mimicry of reconciliation is present in the dynamics of intimate violence. It is, ironically, one of the most dangerous elements of the phenomenon we are exploring. Here we begin to see one of the dynamics disclosed at the mysterious center of the human being: a desire for reunion. Humans long to find relation after violation, and even if they may know that the relationship will continue to be violent, they will often seek some form of reunion instead of isolation. If the fundamental dynamics of intimate violence mock the fundamental goal of the Christian tradition, that is, forgiveness and reconciliation—the formation and re-formation of a community of right relation—then we as a theological and ecclesial community must be very cautious and aware that reconciliation is often misunderstood as reunion. Furthermore, mock reconciliation may intensify future assaults. These dynamics will be discussed in more detail in chapters 4 and 5.

Women remain in this cycle of violence for months, years, even lifetimes. Many people wonder why a woman would stay with a person who beats her. Walker proposes that when women are involved in the cycle of violence, they create survival or coping mechanisms that allow them to have as much control over their environment as possible. As an often-unconscious means of regaining control or a sense of it in their own lives, women adapt their behaviors to the environment of cruelty they are experiencing. This adaptation creates the Battered Woman Syndrome, which evolves out of repeated exposure to trauma in the form of severe abuse or violence, leading to anxiety, hyper-arousal, lowered self-esteem, and a sense of "learned helplessness." Secondary results of this condition are the idealization of the abuser, the denial of danger, and the suppression of appropriate anger.[15] This denial of danger and idealization of the violent partner, coupled with the "contrition" phase of the cycle, can present itself as "reconciliation" to the uninformed ecclesial community.

Referring back to James's story, with which we began this section, we see an example of the repetitive dynamic involved in relationships of intimate violence. A woman with bruises on her face or wrists is not likely a woman who has suffered at the hands of her partner only once; instead, she is the survivor of an ongoing relationship of abuse and a mocking of reconciliation. Even in relationships in which the physical violence is not repeated on a regular basis, intimidation and threats are used to maintain control over the partner.

Power and Control

The Domestic Abuse Intervention Project of Duluth, Minnesota, has developed a curriculum used in educating men about their abusive patterns of control. The program uses a Power and Control Wheel, which contains examples of power and control mechanisms as the "spokes" of the wheel as a heuristic device for understanding the dynamics of intimate violence (see Figure 2). The wheel demonstrates the means through which control and power over a woman may be maintained once a man uses physical violence within the relationship.

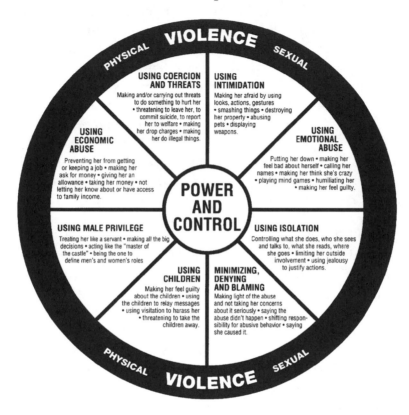

Figure 2. The Power and Control Wheel

Using Intimidation

Making her afraid by using looks, actions, gestures • smashing things • destroying her property • harming pets • displaying weapons • yelling • stalking her • slamming doors • driving recklessly • acting "crazy," "invincible," or like "I have nothing to lose"

Using Emotional Abuse

Putting her down • making her feel bad about herself • calling her names • making her think she's crazy • playing mind games • humiliating her • making her feel guilty • using things that matter to her against her • negatively comparing her to others • having unreasonable demands or expectations • honeymooning her

Using Isolation

Controlling who she sees and talks to, what she reads, where she goes • limiting her outside involvement • using jealousy to justify actions • telling her whom she should trust • interfering with her job • attacking her family • embarrassing her in front of others

Minimizing, Denying, and Blaming

Minimizing • denying • blaming • withholding • omitting • externalizing • distorting • justifying • shifting responsibility • procrastinating • lying

Using Children

Using children to relay messages • using visitation to harass her • threatening to take the children away • using religion to control her • making her feel guilty about her job, her friends, her family, etc. • degrading her about her relationships • abusing the children

Using Male Privilege

Treating her like a servant • making all the decisions • acting like the "master of the castle" • defining men's and women's roles • acting like God • deciding who is responsible for what • deciding who thinks or feels right • being a "know-it-all" • making all of the rules

Using Economic Abuse

Preventing her from getting and keeping a job • making her ask for money • giving her an allowance • not letting her know about or have access to family income • controlling her money • destroying her property • wasting family income • making all financial decisions • forcing her to work to earn income

Using Coercion and Threats

Making and/or carrying out threats to do something to hurt her •
threatening to leave her, to commit suicide, to report her to welfare
• pressuring her to drop charges and/or to do illegal things • threatening negative consequences if she doesn't cooperate • pressuring
her with gifts, promises, apologies

The physical acts of violence function as the rim that holds the
wheel together. These acts of physical and sexual violence hold
the wheel together because they create an ever-present threat
that may be used if intimidation, isolation, or coercion does not
achieve the desired end. At the center of the wheel are power and
control. These two dynamics are understood to be the central
force, that is, they are the power behind the wheel, the engine
that drives the cycle. It is the desire for power and control that
supports all the various behaviors seen in the spokes.

Traumatic Bonding

Donald Dutton, a counselor of abusive men for almost two
decades, claims that when one is discussing intimate violence,
"attachment theory" is a helpful theoretical tool in understanding
why Walker's cycle of violence is explanatory of so many cases.
Using the work of John Bowlby, Dutton claims that the attach-
ments to parental figures in early life can have a deep impact on
the sense of security one feels in future intimate relationships. As
Bowlby states:

> When an individual is confident that an attachment figure will be
> available to him whenever he desires it, that person will be much
> less prone to either intense or chronic fear than the individual
> who for any reason has no such confidence. The second proposi-
> tion concerns the second sensitive period during which such con-
> fidence develops. It postulates that confidence in the availability
> of attachment figures, or lack of it, is built up slowly during the
> years of immaturity—infancy, childhood, adolescence—*and that
> whatever expectations are developed during those years tend to
> persist relatively unchanged throughout the rest of life.*[16]

Dutton finds that studies of abusive men show a correlation between borderline personality organization, attachment disorders, and violence in intimate relationships.[17]

To supplement Walker's theory of Battered Woman Syndrome, Dutton proposes "traumatic bonding" as a description of the dynamic of the woman's felt dependency and idealization of the abuser. Dutton sees the attachment of a woman to her abusive partner as an example of the more common phenomenon that occurs between a child and an abusive parent, a prisoner and a guard, or a hostage and a captor. Traumatic bonding (TB) is defined as "the development of strong emotional ties between two persons, with one person intermittently harassing, beating, threatening, abusing, or intimidating the other."[18]

The dynamics of intimate violence present in all of these models center around the issues of abuse, control, and power. The desire to have power over, or control of, his partner is connected to attachment issues in that the man cannot accept the possibility of being abandoned, and so needs to control his partner. The need for power is also related to patriarchal society, which "demands" from men a sense of power. We will examine this in more detail in the next chapter. When these men feel inadequate, as is often the case, according to Dutton, the need to show that they are not inadequate exhibits itself in the form of abuse and violence. Quoting from Dutton:

> One is reminded of Erich Fromm's definition of sadism as the conversion of feelings of impotence to feelings of omnipotence. While batterers may appear powerful in terms of their physical or sociopolitical resources, they are distinctly impotent in terms of their psychic and emotional resources—even to the point of depending on their female partners to maintain their sense of identity.[19]

What initially appears as contradictory—omnipotence and impotence—instead reveals how the patriarchal culture of dominance turns in on itself. The culture creates an atmosphere in which power over others is so expected that any loss of control is viewed as a sign of impotence and must be compensated for by a turn to physical violence as the most effective or easiest means of reestablishing power over the other.

Figure 3. The Paradox of Power and Control

Presentation of Self to World	*Experience of Self Internally*
Omnipotence	Impotence
Omniscience	Ignorance
"I can handle it"	"I don't think I can handle this"
"I know where I'm going"	"I have no idea where I am or where I am going"
"I am not afraid of anyone"	"I don't want to fight this guy"
"I can always get another job"	"I can't compete in this job market"
"I don't need anyone"	"I need help"

In Figure 3, it is easy to see how this paradox plays itself out in a man's internal struggle. The bravado that we see is often merely a mask to prevent any possibility that someone could question his manhood.

The Abuse of Children by Violent Men

The dynamics addressed above—a desire for power and control, an inability to express emotions other than anger, and a sense of inadequacy that further fuels this anger—are directed not only at a man's partner but also at his children. Though the primary focus of this book is abuse between adults in an intimate relationship, it is important to acknowledge that children are also vulnerable to the effects of male violence. As seen in the Power and Control Wheel (Figure 2), children are often used as a means of punishing or controlling one's partner. Men also become frustrated when they are unable to control their children, and their lack of control often leads to violence toward the "uncontrollable" child. Parenting requires working with a full range of complex emotions, and it leaves even the most fully actualized individuals feeling inadequate before this immense responsibility. Although these dynamics cause most parents to feel overwhelmed and discouraged at times, for the men we have described this type of situation often leads to physical abuse of a child.

It is important for the ecclesial community to recognize that the dynamics that fuel violence against a man's partner are not restricted to that partner. An abused child's mother often attempts to protect her children from abuse, but the opposite may also occur. Children often feel a sense of guilt when their parents fight. In some situations they also try to take the abuse on themselves as a means of protecting their mother. In short, the dynamics of power, control, and violence contribute as much to the abuse of children as they do to the abuse of women.[20] Supporting and challenging violent men to be accountable and nonviolent is a long-term strategy of improving the lives of both children and women.

Stalking
The third and final dynamic of intimate violence, which comes out of the repetitive nature of intimate violence and the subsequent traumatic bonding, is stalking and homicide or suicide. Both the men and the women involved in these relationships experience a feeling of needing each other. Far too often people who know or hear about an abused woman believe she is stupid for staying with an abusive partner. This attitude does not take seriously the danger of leaving or difficulty involved in separating from a partner, even if he is abusive. Women in abusive relationships understand better than anyone else the complexity of their situation. If a community is to be supportive of both men and women in this situation, its members must recognize that a consistent message of support and protection is the most appropriate response to the situation. Patience, endurance, and a compassionate voice serve the entire community.

The proposal to leave her abusive partner is a complex and serious proposal for any woman in a violent relationship. Economic instability, lack of housing, and social isolation make it very difficult for most women to leave an abusive relationship. In addition, when children are a part of the family unit, the woman may want to stay "for the kids." To add to the persuasive factors already stated, most women know they may be at a greater risk of life-threatening abuse if they leave than if they stay with their abuser. According to the National Violence against Women Survey, approximately one million women are stalked annually.[21] A battered woman will often state that her violent partner has said he will find her and kill her if she ever leaves. Because abused women often feel that their abuser is omniscient and omnipotent, the threat of death appears genuine. Statistics also bear out this fear, as they show that there is an increased risk of homicide just after a woman has left her abusive partner.[22]

The abusive man becomes more dangerous when he loses all contact with his partner. There is a sense of urgency for a man when he feels out of control or abandoned. He may even experience this abandonment as a threat to his very existence, so that he feels that regaining control or reestablishing the relationship is a matter of life or death. This is in keeping with Bowlby's research on attachment theory. These dynamics demonstrate the need for an intensive program of intervention by the church community if and when the woman decides to leave her abusive partner.

In her book *Next Time, She'll be Dead*, Ann Jones tells the story of Pamela Guenther, who, after having run away from her abusive husband, started a new relationship with another man and was stalked, threatened, abducted, and eventually killed by her ex-husband. As Jones says:

> Stories like Pamela Guenther's make absorbing TV movies, and reports always "shock and sadden" press and public alike. Often some official board investigates, some official report is issued, and some official wrist is slapped. Some policy is remanded to a committee for further study, and some bereaved relative explains to reporters that the murder victim *did* call the police, she *did* get an order of protection, she *did* leave the man, and yes, she *did* say over and over that he was trying to kill her.[23]

The tone of Jones's book is one of outrage at a system that allows this to occur. But for our purposes, Pamela Guenther's story reminds us that we must realize the duration of the deadly dynamics of intimate violence. (For discussion of the indicators of whether batterers will kill their partner or ex-partner, see Appendix 1.)

The pattern of violence is not just increasingly severe over time. If the relationship is terminated, the woman may need even more support from the community in order to remain safe and provide shelter, food, and education to her children. It is at this point that the church should offer assistance in obtaining an order of protection or a restraining order against the abusive man. Ontario, Canada, has instituted a program of distributing free cellular phones to abused women so that they are able to reach a 911 operator wherever they are. Ideas such as this are the kind of creative, supportive programs that church communities must embrace. Reunion should never be the assumed solution, especially by a church, which often errs on the side of "saving marriages." Instead, reunion of the victim and the violator should be considered only after all precautions for the safety of the survivor are first met.

Equally important is the need for watchful and supportive relationships with the batterers who feel that they are being abandoned one more time. When a woman leaves her abusive partner, the church community should have a group of men and women, trained in the dynamics of intimate violence, who will, for example, stop by to have lunch or dinner with the man. It is important to encourage the man not to begin to stalk his ex-partner. If the man feels that he has other people who care about his well-being and understand the difficulty of losing his partner and children, he may be more likely to succeed in his journey toward nonviolence. The church community has a primary responsibility to assure the batterer that he remains connected to a caring community of support. This community will not only support him but also hold him responsible to the principles found within the gospel of love and respect.

The Possibility of Healing

By examining the dynamics specific to intimate violence, this chapter has highlighted three key features that reconciliation must address and respond to, if it is to be adequate. To heal the wounds of the perpetrator and the survivors of intimate violence, the ecclesial community must realize the multiple levels of violation and enduring dynamics that hinder and limit the potential for successful healing. Reconciliation is not only a symbol of healing for the individual perpetrator, it is a call to vigilance and advocacy for the community. Though healing the individual is a necessary aspect of reconciliation, such healing is only possible with the concomitant healing of the interhuman sphere: the relationship between the partners, the relationship between the perpetrator and his children, and the relationship between the perpetrator and his extended family. In addition to the interhuman sphere, there must be healing on the social level: in the relationship of the perpetrator and the ecclesial community and the healing of the larger society that has been affected by this violation. Further, the individual survivors, especially the violated partner, must be healed. The ecclesial community must also go through a healing process and an ongoing process of conversion toward a greater solidarity with both victims and perpetrators.

The three dynamics addressed in this chapter allow for a realistic proposal of how this healing might be achieved. Through vigilant attention to the techniques used by violent men to control their partners, the ecclesial community can hold men accountable to a nonviolent, nonthreatening, supportive, and contrite lifestyle. By recognizing the cyclical nature of intimate violence, the ecclesial community can be very cautious of any claim that "everything is fine" or "we are more in love than we ever have been." The dynamics of intimate violence endure over time and the "loving contrition" phase of the cycle should not be misunderstood as a genuine stage of healing. Instead, the stage of loving contrition should be understood for what it is, a moment within an ongoing cycle of violence. Finally, the ecclesial community should recognize the seriousness of its role as healer of violent relationships. The potential for torture, murder, and suicide is a chilling reminder of the importance of a responsible and safe approach to intimate violence. The classic symbol of reconciliation must recognize that the healing of these wounds is difficult and dangerous work. The scars left behind by violence may never completely heal, and reconciliation should not attempt to hide the ugliness of the scars. The violations are real, and they often leave both partners in the relationship broken. Reconciliation, if it is to be a genuine symbol of hope, one that reveals the divine in and through history, must recognize its role as a gentle and demanding healer. The ecclesial community must be willing to work through periods of despair, rejection, anger, and pain.

We have addressed the basic dynamics of intimate violence in this chapter. It is now necessary to delve deeper into the roots of violence, especially male violence, and this will be the goal of the second chapter. Together, the first two chapters will present a clear and challenging picture of the violence found within families and compel us to develop an ecclesial response to this violence.

2

Violence:
Destruction of the Mysterious Human Center

In every human being, of course, there lurks a beast uncontrollable, unleashed from the chain, a beast of ailments contracted in debauchery.   DOSTOYEVSKY, *The Brothers Karamozov*

Violence has the capacity to diminish, degrade, and destroy life. Domestic violence, as we saw in chapter 1, is not a one-time act but a cyclical pattern of behavior that creates a complex bond between the perpetrator and the victim. The relationship's intensity and complexity demand extreme caution on the part of persons who attempt to advocate for those suffering from the violence. The current chapter will address the question of how our society understands violence and how societal structures condone violence in general and intimate violence in particular. Through this understanding we move more deeply into the phenomenon that the symbol of reconciliation claims to overcome. Without a full appreciation of the seriousness of violence, a claim to reconciliation acts only as a veneer and does not penetrate the surface. This chapter attempts to uncover some of the key contributing factors to male violence.

Cultural Influences on Violent Men

Focusing on the specific behaviors and dynamics of violent men helps us to understand and begin to develop models for addressing the healing of these men and their many relationships. Yet it is also important to address the larger cultural picture, not only as a means of understanding violent men and their partners and children, but more significantly understanding how all of us are

influenced by a culture that condones violence, embraces patriarchy, and dismisses the possibilities of healing and hope that this
book espouses.

In the social ethics class I teach, I offered the following true
scenario to a group of twenty-five college juniors and seniors.

> On February 17, 1994, Kenneth Peacock, a thirty-six-year-old
> long-distance truck driver, returned home unexpectedly because
> of a snowstorm and found his wife in bed with another man. The
> enraged Peacock chased the other man out of the house at gun-
> point. After several hours of drinking and arguing with his
> unfaithful wife, Peacock shot her with a hunting rifle.
>
> As punishment for killing his wife in cold blood, Baltimore,
> Maryland, Judge Robert E. Cahill gave Peacock an eighteen-
> month jail sentence and ordered him to perform fifty hours of
> community service in a domestic-violence program. Judge Cahill
> expressed reluctance in having to sentence Peacock at all, stating
> that he gave him a prison sentence only "to keep the system hon-
> est." "I seriously wonder," Cahill said at the sentencing, "how many
> married men—married five, four years—would have the strength
> to walk away without inflicting some corporal punishment."[1]

When asked to break into groups and decide whether the judge's
sentence was appropriate, the majority of men and women felt
that the judge's sentence was completely inappropriate and
should have been more severe. In contrast to this large group,
there was also a group of about five men, almost half of the men
in this class, who felt that any man would have done what the man
did in this scenario. One of the students said, "If I come into *my*
house and find someone sleeping with *my* wife, in *my* bed, someone's going to get killed." Other men agreed.

What was hopeful was that the majority of men in the class
claimed that the husband had no right to assault or kill the man or
his own wife. The five men who felt they had a right to harm their
partners represent the cultural heritage of patriarchy and voice
approval of violence toward women. Most men recognize that, as
angry as they might become when confronted with a situation of
infidelity, the law does not allow them to respond violently to the

situation. The question is, how should society address the one-third to one-half of men who believe that they have a right to punish their spouse and the other man? Another question is, how does society respond to a judge who believes any "normal" man would punish his wife in the same situation?

Are the reactions of the men in my class, the judge on the bench, and Mr. Peacock a matter of cultural conditioning or genetic susceptibility? It would appear that there might be a combination of inherited and learned characteristics at play in these men. Patriarchal culture, which has in recent years been put under scrutiny,[2] has clearly supported men's ownership rights over their spouses and children. Laws have changed dramatically from the early 1800s to now. Assaulting one's wife has moved from being expected and legitimate behavior to being illegal. The Supreme Court of Mississippi ruled in favor of corporal punishment of one's spouse in 1824,[3] and it was not until the late 1800s in many states that beating one's wife was made illegal.

> In 1871 wife beating was made illegal in Alabama. The court stated: The privilege, ancient though it be, to beat her with a stick, to pull her hair, choke her, spit in her face or kick her about the floor, or to inflict upon her like indignities, is not now acknowledged by our law. . . . The wife is entitled to the same protection of the law that the husband can invoke for himself.[4]

Yet there remain judges, like Judge Cahill in Maryland, who find in certain circumstances exonerations of violence against a spouse.[5]

It is not only the legal system and the courts that must be understood: marketing now carries contradictory messages into every living room. Many advertisements continue to reinforce the typical male stereotypes of the man in charge of the household, while others focus on the independence and power of women in today's society. Some of the most interesting and successful commercials are those that play on this ambiguity in our culture and point out clearly the struggle between men and women over the transition from patriarchal ways of power distribution to a shared model of power distribution.

The question we now need to raise is, What are the ongoing influences of our culture? How do these voices, symbols, and practices help men to minimize and deny their own violence? Does the culture support women and children in their difficult journey out of a violent home? What areas of culture do most people accept without question as they interact with their neighbors, parishioners, clients, and family members? What is the source of violence, and how can we understand its role in society? All of these questions are vital for churches to consider if they wish to be prophetic voices for the vulnerable in society.

Are Men Inherently Violent Creatures?

Analysis of violence begins with a brief examination of the proposal that violence is necessary or instinctual in men. If this proposal is true, then there is little hope for conversion and rehabilitation of the violent men discussed in chapter 1. It is important to recognize the overwhelming evidence that men commit more violent crimes. The FBI's 2000 Uniform Crime Report states that 82.6 percent of all those arrested for violent crime were men. In the same year men accounted for 98.9 percent of those arrested for forcible rape.[6] These numbers do not suggest a slight trend of men being more criminally violent than women but an overwhelmingly consistent pattern. This is something all men must come to terms with; for the sake of our sons and daughters, we must attempt to understand the correlation between masculinity and violence.

Scarcely could one begin to talk about intimate relationships and violence and not address the influence (or obstacle, as the case may be) that Sigmund Freud laid upon the collective consciousness of the twentieth century. If one attends to Freud's conversation on the connection between erotic love and violence in *Civilization and Its Discontents,* one finds a theory of the human being as a hungry wolf.[7] Freud identifies the underlying nature of humans as *homo homini lupus* and finds that an instinctual desire to be a wolf toward others is part of our given "nature."

The bit of truth behind all this—*one so eagerly denied*—is that men are not gentle, friendly creatures wishing for love, who simply defend themselves if they are attacked, but that a powerful measure of desire for aggression has to be reckoned as part of their instinctual endowment. The result is that their neighbor is to them not only a possible helper or sexual object, but also a temptation to them to gratify their aggressiveness on him, to exploit his capacity for work without recompense, to use him sexually without his consent, to seize his possessions, to humiliate him, to cause him pain, to torture and to kill him.[8]

Freud believed that humans view each other as objects of desire. We wish to use the other person to satisfy our sexual desires, and we also wish to use the other person as a means of satisfying our need for violence. Freud believed that we are gratified when we act violently.

The Hydraulic Model

Myriam Miedzian analyzes several theories of why men are violent in her book *Boys Will Be Boys*. Though she disagrees with Freud's theory of why humans, especially males, are violent, she does show how influential Freud's theory has become in explaining violence. Miedzian refers to Freud's theory as the "hydraulic model" in which aggression is like "a fluid constantly applying pressure against the walls of its containers."[9] Understood in this way, the need to be violent can only be suppressed for a certain period of time, after which one explodes in a violent rage. The model has been persuasive to many people in our society, because it appears to explain the feelings we express with phrases like, "I am going to explode!" and "I have had it up to here!" The problem with this model lies in its inability to address the complex character of the human being. Some people appear to have very little or no aggressive drive, while others become violent in almost any emotional situation.

Another inadequacy of the hydraulic model is that it does not take seriously the gendered character of violence. Men are far more likely to be violent in every arena of life. Men have done the vast majority of killing in wars throughout history. Men are far more likely to commit violent crimes. Men are more likely to use physical aggression when they become angry.[10] Given these cultural facts, it is necessary to develop an understanding of violence that addresses the reasons why men are more likely to be violent than women. A theory of violence must take gendered differences seriously; we will briefly discuss the importance of gender below so that we can begin to address the way in which society and the church can appropriately respond to instances of intimate violence.

One important difference between men and women is the way men are socialized to react to their emotional world. Many psychologists and social scientists have recognized that the one feeling men are most comfortable expressing is anger. The full spectrum of emotions is funneled into this one emotion for many men. This handicaps men in terms of the lack of a rich emotional life, and it also endangers those around them. If feelings of inadequacy, disappointment, sadness, embarrassment, and grief all become anger and rage, the family members and friends of men are almost always pushed away instead of being invited to console the sad or grieving man. This is an aspect of socialization and can be seen in the way boys are trained to express their emotions. Figure 4 demonstrates this phenomenon in terms of an emotional funnel, where all of the different emotions going into the funnel are finally expressed in terms of anger.

Part of what feeds the hydraulic theory is the funneling of emotions into anger. What Freud offers is a theory of violence that assumes the need to be violent. It is relevant to this study primarily because it is accepted by so many men in our culture as the explanation for their violence. If we, as the ecclesial community, can find an alternative to the hydraulic model, we can refute the assumption that violence is necessary.

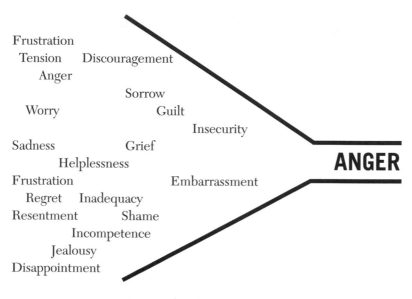

Figure 4. The Emotional Funnel

It is also essential in work with boys and men to expand their repertoire of emotional literacy and understanding. Naming the emotions is one of the first steps in creating emotional literacy for young boys, and emotional literacy in boys may lead to less expressed anger in male adolescents and in men. One important task of this volume is to show that violence, especially violence in intimate relationships, is not necessary. It is, rather, a response to stimuli that have their roots in cultural expectations, societal acceptance, and personal history. No one factor, especially not biological instinct or a psychic drive, mandates that humans be violent; therefore, humans have the capacity to move beyond violence if they find communities of solidarity, resistance, and support.

A Girardian Interpretation of Violence

A second theory of violence, which also influences us in our initial reactions to and explanations of violence, is that of René Girard. Girard focuses attention on the underlying motivation for violence, which he sees as revenge initiated by *mimesis*. Girard claims that mimetic violence is based in the desire to have what one's mentor or role model has. Once a boy begins to want what his father, teacher, or coach has, the stage is set for a conflict over the desired object. The struggle can be resolved through an infinite regression of vengeance or by the introduction of a scapegoat. The scapegoat functions to turn the violence of both parties away from each other and toward a third party. Girard's theory claims that violence, in fact, is the stabilizing factor in the formation of all human community. In his work *Violence and the Sacred*, Girard proposes sacrifice as the explanatory event that channels the need for vengeance into appropriate, and even sacred, rituals.[11] According to Girard, violence, understood ritually, is a necessary practice that keeps the rest of the community safe. All the destructive violence that would be taken out on other members of the community is channeled through the ritual killing or scapegoating of one person or animal. This brings the community together instead of tearing it apart.

Girard places acts of violence into two categories: reciprocal violence and sacrificial or sacred violence.[12] Reciprocal violence is done toward another member of the community in revenge for a previous act of violence. If reciprocal violence is left undisturbed, it destroys the entire community, because each act of violence calls forth another. Sacred violence is ritualized violence used as a means of reconciling the community to itself. Sacred violence eliminates the need for any reciprocal violence, because the desire for revenge has been channeled into the killing of the sacrificial victim.[13] Girard is similar to Freud in his proposal that humans "must" be violent, but for a different reason. According to his theory, it is not because we have an instinctual drive toward violence, but because we cannot avoid our desire for vengeance. It is this very truth that is exposed in the sacred violence. Note the connection here to the case of Kenneth Peacock, earlier in this chapter. Without a sacrifice, which releases the desire for vengeance, complete societal disintegration would follow. As Girard states, "The desire to commit an act of violence on those near us cannot be suppressed without a conflict; we must divert that impulse, therefore, toward the sacrificial victim, the creature we can strike down without fear of reprisal, since he [sic] lacks a champion."[14] Girard sees the human community involved in "an interminable, infinitely repetitive process."[15] This perpetual desire for revenge can only be held at bay through the communal sacrifice, which Girard refers to as "sacred violence."

Ready to Snap like a Mousetrap

One final model that is influential in contemporary notions of why humans act violently comes from E. O. Wilson. Wilson, a sociobiologist, attempts to understand human behavior from an evolutionary standpoint and through current biological data. He softens the Freudian model by claiming that aggression is not a necessary drive that must be discharged on a regular basis. Instead, Wilson sees aggression as a predisposition that is "wired" into human beings. Wilson turns, as it were, from a hydraulic model to a "mousetrap" model of violence.[16] He claims that we are always-already capable of acting violently if the situation stimulates certain emotional or relational conditions. We inherit a chemical substructure that can be easily activated when we feel out of control, threatened, or powerless. As Wilson states:

> Aggressive behavior, especially in its more dangerous forms of military action and criminal assault, is learned. But the learning is prepared. . . . We are strongly predisposed to slide into deep, irrational hostility under certain definable conditions. With dangerous ease, hostility feeds on itself and ignites runaway reactions that can swiftly progress to alienation and violence.[17]

Wilson and Girard both show a subtle move away from the instinctual model of Freud and toward a more relational model. The more relational model argues for an inherent capacity for violence activated by external stimuli or triggered if the right conditions arise. In Girard's case, it becomes a need for revenge once the first act of violence has occurred. For Wilson, it is a hardwired capacity for violence, which is not necessarily activated by any one specific phenomenon but remains always at the ready and is engaged in different people and groups by multifaceted stimuli.

In this model, humans are like living adjustable mousetraps, set at their conception and made more sophisticated through their maturation. The mousetrap model suggests that humans are prone to react to certain stimuli with violence. At the same time, the mousetrap may sit unsprung for a lifetime, if the stimuli never present themselves. Additionally, because the mousetrap is always evolving physiologically, psychologically, and culturally within each person, the stimuli vary from trap to trap, and each trap has the capacity to change over time. The trigger mechanism may require an almost imperceptible touch in one case and a hammer-like blow in another. The ability to modify the sensitivity of the trigger mechanism opens the human to the possibility of self-transcendence. We may all be initially wired with different sensitivities that make us more or less likely to act on our innate potential for violence. The goal of a society might then be to understand the mechanism and continually to desensitize the trap, in some respects to rust the trap so that it becomes so insensitive to its wiring that it becomes almost unable to react with violence under any stimuli.[18]

Gender and Violence

What is the role of gender, and how does society influence boys to become more violent than girls? These are important questions to pose in light of the ideas of Freud, Girard, and Wilson about violence. Myriam Miedzian, summarizing her findings from the research she did for *Boys Will Be Boys,* states, "We must begin to move beyond a simplistic view of violence in which one side contends that it is biological and therefore nothing can be done about it, while the other side asserts that human beings are naturally good and violence is caused by socialization alone."[19] As we have noted above, the propensity to violence lies not only in biology or psychology but also in socialization and culture.

What do boys receive from culture and biology that leads them, as a group, to be more violent than girls? Miedzian offers four possible explanations: (1) Higher levels of testosterone may lead to a lower threshold for frustration in boys. (2) Boys tend to be treated more roughly, and this reinforces any desire for dominance. (3) Disabilities occur more frequently in boys than in girls. And (4) peer pressure to prove manhood through fighting is culturally endorsed.[20] Stephen Boyd expands on Miedzian's last point as he describes the pressures associated with growing up male. Boyd develops a chart in his book *The Men We Long to Be* in which he demonstrates the ways in which society reinforces antisocial and destructive aggression in boys and men.[21] Reinforcement of aggression comes through societal cues in the physical, emotional, sexual, intellectual, and relational areas of our lives. Boys and men hear over and over again that they are a "wimp" or a "sissy," a "fag" or a "queer." Boyd constructs a compelling argument for how boys are molded through a "gender dance" into men who are more likely to approach women in a state of desperation. Men are emotionally and relationally challenged when they develop according to the traditional "gender dance," and often this leads through the emotional funnel described in Figure 4 to anger and, finally, to violence. Both men and women are challenged by these stereotypes. The behaviors most discouraged in boys are stereotypically feminine behaviors.

One can see in the chart developed by Boyd that a man is understood to be a true man through his public portrayal of his masculinity. This involves strength, power, and control. If a man does not live up to his publicly expected role as strong, he is labeled a wimp or a sissy. These are societal enforcers, in that they motivate men to reestablish themselves as strong and in control. These enforcers come through peer groups, generational expectations, and modeling of violent behavior on television, movies, and computer games.

Media and Violence

A clear connection has been demonstrated between television viewing and violent behavior. The National Institute of Mental Health, in its 1982 annual report, concludes: "The consensus among most of the research community is that violence on television does lead to aggressive behavior by children and teenagers who watch the programs. . . . In magnitude, television violence is as strongly correlated with aggressive behavior as any other behavioral variable that has been measured."[22] Little doubt remains that violence in society and depicted in the media affects children, and this violence carries forward into adult life.[23] Once patterns of behaviors and social norms are internalized, occurring primarily between the ages of four and twelve, the adjustment of these societal expectations becomes more and more difficult. Boys see men fighting in movies and on television. Boys also play out their own violent fantasies in computer and video games. A boy can kill thousands of villains in one afternoon without breaking a sweat. Can girls also play these video games and watch these movies? Yes, but they are not culturally reinforced. In fact, it is just the opposite: social enforcers, such as "tomboy," "uppity," and "bitch," are used when girls take on more aggressive traits.[24] The violence observed and played out reinforces the traits in Boyd's scheme.

Another arena in which boys are socialized to be tough and violent is sports. It is most easily identifiable in boxing, hockey, and football, but the strong, silent, macho, tough-guy attitude can be found in most sporting activities for boys. Sports endorse the myth of masculinity. It is often in the locker room that boys are first exposed to the social enforcers that Boyd has described. The weak one is often picked out and ridiculed to emphasize to other boys that they should not be like him, since "he's a fag." This behavior becomes a part of the male code and creates a situation in which any boy who shows nurturing behavior for those picked on by the bullies is also labeled a "wuss," a "fag," or a "queer." One sees here another form of the scapegoating mechanism described by Girard. Those who refuse to be aggressive will become scape-goats for the rest of the aggressive males.

Some excellent coaches support each player in his personal development, but many coaches look the other way, allowing certain players to become scapegoats for the team. In fact, many coaches endorse degrading locker-room banter as a part of what it means to become a man. In college and high school sports, hazing is often a part of the ritual of becoming a member of the team. All of these behaviors create an environment in which the feelings of vulnerability, frustration, inadequacy, and fear are funneled into the one socially approved emotion of anger. The anger is not to be taken out on one's teammates, so it is often expressed with a girlfriend that afternoon or at a party that evening. The incidence of dating violence is a serious problem in many high schools.[25] It is an issue that most parents, coaches, clergy, and counselors are unwilling or unequipped to address.

Interpreting Violence as Constructive or Destructive

Besides understanding the cultural and personal roots of violence and theories of its origin, we must acknowledge and understand that its effects are both positive and negative. Its ability to interpret violence as constructive or destructive remains one of society's most powerful tools. The very existence of violence is dependent on a complex web of prior conceptual understandings and definitions. All violent events, as violent, draw on the distinction between order and disorder.[26] Violence has as its first defining characteristic a breaching of the socially accepted view of what is civil or appropriate. Violence violates predefined social limits. The primary distinction between constructive and destructive violence involves the ends to which the act is aimed: "Destructive violence is generally understood to be violence employed toward non-creative, negative ends. . . . Constructive violence is violence . . . employed toward creative, positive ends."[27] This is similar to the distinction made by Girard between sacred violence and destructive violence. The central problem is who perceives or defines the claim to creative, positive ends or noncreative, negative ends.

Distinguishing between destructive violence and constructive violence is at the core of ideas such as just war, self-defense, and revolution. A woman who kills her abusive partner may be an example of constructive violence when it is an instance of self-defense. Though the church community cannot endorse homicide as an appropriate response to battering, the tradition has always made distinctions between violence used in defense of the innocent and violence used by an aggressor to destroy the innocent. A woman who kills her partner or husband because she can no longer watch him brutalize their children or bear further abuse herself is certainly in a situation that must be examined through a unique hermeneutical lens. All situations of "constructive violence" depend on the validity of a socially constructed distinction between destructive and constructive violence.[28]

Crime and Punishment: Constructive or Destructive Violence?

Criminal behavior includes the most universally accepted instances of destructive violence. People found guilty of destructive violence are designated criminal and unfit to function in society and so are removed. The criminal justice system is designed in part to "handle" those who represent a danger to society. Violent people are incarcerated in order to deny them the means and opportunity to harm anyone else. But does this mechanism, the most basic means by which society addresses the problem of violent men, actually help? Or does it create more violent men?

It is important to note, before examining how the criminal justice system affects men, that the criminal justice system does need to be a part of the solution to domestic violence. In spite of all its flaws, it is essential to have a system that can incarcerate certain men at specific times of their lives in order to provide some level of protection for their partners and children. Without the ability to be assured that a man is no longer able to harm a woman and her children, cases similar to that of Pamela Guenther, discussed at the end of chapter 1, are always a possibility. That said, I wish to show that the criminal justice system as it stands today is a grossly inadequate system to address the issue of reconciling the batterer with the larger community and, potentially, with his family.

In the year 2000, the number of people incarcerated in the United States reached a remarkable two million people. That is, one in every 130 people in the country was incarcerated. This number has continued to rise as a percentage of the population. The percentage of people in prison has doubled between 1985 and 1996. During this time period, the total number of inmates rose from just under 750,000 to over 1.6 million.[29] We are building prisons at a breakneck pace to keep up with more than 8 percent annual growth in the prison population. If prisons were performing their task of helping to rehabilitate men, the money would be well spent. But instead the opposite is the case. Men make up more than 90 percent of the prison population in the United States, and they are more often than not demeaned and violated within the prison system.

James Gilligan, a psychiatrist who has worked in the court system as well as inside prisons, claims in his book *Violence: Reflections on a National Epidemic* that violent men are motivated by justice and "self-protection" and that they have low self-esteem and shame as primary motivators in their violent behavior.[30] This claim does not diminish the claim made in chapter 1 that the desire for power and control is a primary motivation in men who are violent with their partners; rather, it nuances this description by deepening the understanding of one of the causes behind the desire for power and control. Gilligan distinguishes between two "hermeneutical stances" toward violent behavior, one that focuses on the world as a "morality play" and the other, which interprets the world as a "tragedy." Gilligan uses a tragic hermeneutic as his guiding lens. When we experience and interpret our world as a morality play, he argues, we are always trying to identify the perpetrators and clearly distinguish them from the victims. Punishing the perpetrators and protecting the victims is the means toward achieving justice. In contrast, seeing the same set of circumstances primarily as tragedy recognizes that the lines between those who inflict violence and those who suffer from violence are far more blurry and ambiguous than a "morality play" can allow. Gilligan claims that, from the perspective of the violent offender, violence is a means to achieve justice:

> The first lesson that tragedy teaches (and that the morality play misses) is that *all violence is an attempt to achieve justice*, or what the violent person perceives as justice, for himself or for whoever it is on whose behalf he is acting. . . . Thus, *the attempt to achieve and maintain justice, or to undo or prevent injustice, is the one and only universal cause of violence.*[31]

Gilligan's basic presupposition also informs classical philosophy and Christian theological anthropology. From the works of Aristotle through Thomas Aquinas and into the work of Karl Rahner, one finds affirmation that all creation is good and all actions are directed at some good. The aim of the act may be perverted or misdirected in some way, but from the perspective of the doer, the action is always directed at some good. In this way, Gilligan's proposal is basically an Aristotelian criminological analysis: all the men he encounters attempt to achieve justice, a good, but often their means of achieving justice are brutally violent.

Many in the criminal justice system would agree with this assessment. However, they would also caution that a small percentage of violent offenders are simply predators. These predators might also be trying to achieve some form of justice or some good, but their fundamental stance in the world entails taking advantage of the weak and vulnerable whenever possible. This group is different from most of the people who end up within the criminal justice system. Though batterers may all appear to be predators, my experience working with these violent men suggests that only a small percentage of them present predatory behavior. I believe it is important always to attempt to distinguish between predatory men and those who are influenced by their familial and social surroundings to expect power and control in the relationship.

Gilligan proposes revising our understanding of violence. He attempts to prevent future violence by exposing the penal system's use of punishment (destructive violence).[32] Through increasing the factors that cause violence, the criminal justice system does not ameliorate, but instead worsens, the violence already present in our society. Gilligan claims that:

> Punishment is a form of violence in its own right—albeit a legally sanctioned form—but it is also the cause of violence, as it stimulates the very same illegal violence that it ostensibly intended to inhibit or prevent. . . . Punishment stimulates violence; punishment causes it. The more punitive our society has become, the higher our rate of violence (both criminal and non-criminal) has become.[33]

In fact, Gilligan sees the entire social system as reinforcing violent behavior and worsening violence in the name of justice and the public good. Clearly one can see connections among Gilligan's critique of societal violence and the *ahimsa* doctrine of nonviolence espoused by Mohandas K. Gandhi and the nonviolent civil disobedience advanced by Martin Luther King, Jr.. Nonviolence is not new to Christian reflection, but it has certainly been lost sight of in our relation to criminals. This is true in part simply because we do not visit people in prison, as the gospel calls us to do. If we did visit people in prison on a regular basis, we might understand the system better and work more fervently to reform it. We might also be able to see more readily that the prison system functions as a societal scapegoating system.

The idea that violent men have low self-esteem may at first seem absurd. Violence is, after all, self-assertion, and the men one encounters in domestic-violence courtrooms seem anything but timid, quiet, or shy. These characteristics, often associated with low self-esteem, are absent from the public personas of these men. I believe this is a gendered definition of self-esteem. In females, it may be that low self-esteem is exhibited through behaviors of shyness, timidity, and quietness. On the other hand, in men, who have been taught to mask their sense of inadequacy, a tendency exists to be arrogant, conceited, and filled with "pride" when they are actually feeling insecure and worthless. False pride masks genuine self-hate and low self-esteem. These feelings can then become manifest in violence, again due to the emotional funnel described in Figure 4.

Gilligan claims that, though not all violent men are victims of violence themselves, many are survivors of emotionally or physically abusive childhoods. When violence is inflicted on another human being, it leads to a sense of humiliation and shame. This is no less true of these men than it is of their victims.

Gilligan goes so far as to state that society as a whole, and especially members of its upper class, perpetuate violence for their own self-interest. He does not use René Girard's work explicitly, but he is making a Girard-like critique. Gilligan maintains that social stratification in our society is employed by the upper class to maintain its position of economic and political power over the rest of society, and one key to this social stratification is the maintenance of a violent underclass:

> What is it about our social class system that holds in place a self-defeating policy of increasingly violent punishment, when we have clearly demonstrated that such policies stimulate violence? A society's prisons serve as a key for understanding the larger society as a whole. . . . It is worth noting that the rulers of any society, just like the prison guards, have an interest in pursuing the strategies I have described earlier: "You scratch my back, I'll scratch yours" and "Divide and conquer."[34]

It is through the "war on crime" that relative stability is maintained for the upper class. Is it not the case that we continue to incarcerate more and more criminals, building more prisons (which make the middle class feel safer), while at the same time we reduce the capital gains tax? We do not focus on programs like prenatal nutrition or Head Start with the same vigor as we do the war on crime because they are "too expensive." Gilligan lists eleven social policies that contribute to the maintenance of legally defined "crime" and violence while at the same time continuing to oppress the lower class as a whole. These policies endorse punishment and increase poverty, and so increase social stratification, with a net result of an increase in violence within our society.[35]

Ironically, then, both the perpetrator and society foment violence in a twisted pursuit of justice. This social analysis of violence in America dramatically highlights the distortion of our desire for justice and right relation, which is implicit in any desire for communal living. Certainly the church's role is to challenge these self-destructive social policies, as well as to work with individuals and local criminal justice systems. The liberation of violent men from their cycle of destructiveness through their reconciliation to a community of responsibility and care is the prophetic stand that the ecclesial community must take in our contemporary society. It is through responsible healing of violent men that we also advance the liberation of women and children who have suffered from their violence.

The Warnings Offered by Violence

Three basic ideas have been examined in this chapter. First, we have claimed that the potential to be violent is an inherent constitutive element of being human. Second, we have proposed that all understandings of violence are relative to the socially constructed meanings of "constructive violence" and "destructive violence." Finally, we have seen that violence is a socially endorsed phenomenon maintained through the dehumanization of those who commit acts of violence. These affirmations have specific consequences that any adequate response to violence must take into account.

Freud, Girard, and Wilson present an anthropology that suggests humanity will always be violent. Their visions of an inherently violent dimension within humans must be criticized or modified but also factored into any anthropology that attempts to understand human violence. To hold violent men responsible, society and the ecclesial community must understand the models of violence that have informed and shaped the cultural explanations for responses to violence.

The ecclesial community must also take seriously the insights offered by a linguistic analysis of violence. If the way violence is defined depends on the understanding of order, society, and culture, then the church's response to violence must recognize its own participation in the formulation of what is defined as "violence." Understandings of "constructive violence" and "destructive violence" in the United States of America and Western Europe are, to a large part, products of the Western Christian definitional structure. If the ecclesial community can confront its heritage as a collaborator in the condoning of violence, it may better understand its responsibility in healing and minimizing the continuation of violence.

Finally, the idea that the very institution designed to mitigate the consequence of violence, the criminal justice system, in fact perpetuates violence seriously challenges any proposal designed to heal relationships affected by violence. Reconciliation as a Christian symbol of healing, for example, must recognize that violence is not removed through dehumanizing the perpetrator. The dehumanization and humiliation of the perpetrator only serve to exacerbate the problem. Therefore reconciliation, if it is to respond adequately to intimate violence, must recognize the full humanity of both the perpetrator and the survivor.

This chapter takes us one step further in our goal of understanding violence so that we might begin to heal men who are violent. Three insights help us to understand the nature of violence more clearly: First, from the works of Freud, Girard, and Wilson we discover that deep psychological, social, and biological factors prepare humans to be violent. Second, Miedzian and Boyd show that this preparation is reinforced and channeled to support boys and men when they act out this potential for aggression. And third, the culture aggravates this aggressive tendency among men by the way it seeks to punish those who act out violently. We now have a clear appreciation for the paradoxical nature of intimate violence and the breadth and depth of the cultural support for male violence. In the next chapter we turn to the complicating role that religion plays in the cultural support of domestic violence. One would wish to see Christianity standing as a firm and clear prophetic voice against the trends uncovered in the first two chapters, but to the contrary, we will discover in chapter 3 that Christianity has not tried to rust the mousetrap or douse the fires of violence within the family. Instead, it has more often than not subtly fanned the flames of intimate violence.

3

Does Christianity Throw Gas on the Flames of Violence?

For days after the wedding,
she left the balloon heart
hanging on her car's antenna.
She liked the way the limp
bubble drooped and bounced
each day becoming emptier,
heavier, less like a celebration.
After three weeks it snowed.
By then the heart had slid down
until it touched the hood,
and as she drove, the thing,
now frozen, knocked and knocked
like knuckles on a hard wood desk,
like an ice pick chipping away.

BETH GYLYS

Violent men live in our communities and belong to our parishes. What do we, as churches, say to them? How does Christianity support and protect women and children? Does Christianity hold violent men responsible? The clear answer to these questions at this point in history is that Christianity has, more often than not, added fuel to the flames of violence within the home rather than doused the fire. Christianity has claimed that marriages should continue regardless of their circumstances. Christian theology has endorsed patriarchal roles for men. Church leaders have often colluded with abusive men, minimizing and denying the abuse they see, to the detriment of the women and children in their parish. This chapter will examine Christian marriage as a lens through which one can initially see the church's subtle support of

47

violent relationships. I will also examine the images of the divine used by the church and the ways in which these support men's desire to be in control of their partners, lovers, and children. The Christian community embraces powerful symbols of liberation and responsibility. It should not use these symbols to further the abuse of women and children but rather as a clear voice in support of women and children—and the men who abuse them.

The Classic Symbol of Marriage

The shared symbolic history of any given society deeply influences each member of that society. Accepted linguistic and cultural standards shape the way humans relate to one another, to their institutions, and even to themselves. For these reasons, an analysis of the deeply rooted Christian symbol of marriage helps us gain perspective on the obstacles that must be overcome in rearticulating reconciliation. The deep symbolic importance of marriage—which rises to the level of sacrament in some traditions—cannot be underestimated, especially as it relates to the way in which reconciliation may appropriately respond to relationships of intimate violence. One primary cultural legacy of the sacrament of marriage is found in the words "for better or for worse." These words, though seemingly benign, can function within a violent relationship as a religious restraint against leaving an abusive partner. In this chapter we seek to uncover the roots of the cultural and religious expectations associated with marriage, for example, that reunion is always preferable to separation. This and other common beliefs have had an impact on the meaning and use of reconciliation within the cultural and ecclesial symbol structure.

As discussed in chapter 1, David Tracy claims that classic symbols endure over time and, though ambiguous, do have the capacity to disclose meaning and truth. And what is it about marriage or violence that endures and haunts us? The very possibility of a relationship's enduring throughout one's adult life has the potential to challenge and transform each person in the couple. Marriage confronts and provokes by its claim that in fact two people can be committed to a relationship that can endure over time and create a network of new relationships through friendship and procreation. The endurance of marriage is its most provocative feature. Is it not absurd to commit to another human being at one point and expect, or even claim, at that moment, that one is sure that this relationship will endure "for better or for worse"? The symbol of marriage has existed since the code of Hammarabi and likely before, and though it has changed dramatically over the last six thousand years, it has primarily been a symbol of enduring relationship involving commitment, family, and possibly love.[1] The symbol remains ambiguous, however, since it has also meant possession, slavery, subordination, and social stratification.

A fundamental mystery attaches to the symbol of marriage. Marriage has the capacity to inspire new forms of relationship. One sees in demands that committed same-sex couples be allowed to marry or that Catholic priests never be allowed to marry the ongoing discussion over the meaning and power of the classic symbol of marriage. In this chapter, we will also examine the connections between marriage and violence. Without a clear understanding of the ambiguity that resides in the sedimented religious cultural appropriations of the term *marriage* and its connections to *violence,* one cannot begin to deconstruct and then reconstruct the symbol of reconciliation.

The Marriage of Hosea

To begin our analysis of the symbol of marriage, we turn to a biblical marriage that functions as a symbol of the divine-human relationship and also involves violence. The Hebrew Bible not only offers clear models of marriage, especially in conjunction with the history of the covenant with the patriarchs and the people of Israel, it also exemplifies how the covenant between Yahweh and Israel was a model for the marriage covenant, and vice versa. In this respect, Yahweh's violence came to legitimate spousal violence. In the prophetic literature of the divided kingdoms of

Israel and Judah, for example, violence is used to punish the "wicked" or "adulterous" wife. The prophet Hosea beats his adulterous wife in order to bring her back to him, and the book raises this as an analogy to Yahweh's punishment of his "spouse," Israel. Reconciliation is understood as reunion, not the reestablishment of a relationship to a community.[2] The "beating" that Israel symbolically endures is a punishment for its infidelity to Yahweh. Yahweh/Hosea look forward to a renewed relationship after the beating is over. The punishment is just a part of the cycle of violation that continues between Yahweh and Israel. As Renita Weems summarizes the poetry of Hosea: "Marital strife has given way to harmony, and accusations have dissolved into *reconciliation*. Thus the audience has been invited to ponder the imponderable. Those who once were condemned for their shameless disloyalty to God are now promised that after an obligatory period of punishment there remains the possibility of restoration."[3] Marriage and even rape are thus used, in the Book of Hosea, as in Ezekiel and Jeremiah, as metaphors for the relationship between God and God's people. The appropriate response to infidelity is chastisement and punishment. Marriage is twisted into a symbolic medium through which the cultural expectation of reunion and obedience is delivered to the Israelites.

Historical Christian Interpretations of Marriage

Marriage was taken from Judaism into Christianity as one of the central religious realities and symbols of the divine-human relationship, though in this transition the early Christians introduced an anti-family sentiment that had both ascetic and eschatological roots.[4] A gradual move toward a family-centered religion occurred slowly and was consistently challenged by the notion of the superiority of the celibate life. With the Protestant Reformation in the sixteenth century, a clear and decisive turn recognized family as central to Christianity. Reformation thinkers sought to "unify the church and the family by insisting that marriage was a creational ordinance demanded of all, as well as a necessary means to control the urges of fallen 'man.'"[5] The maintenance of order remained central in the marriage system. One can see this in the following text from that time:

> So punish your wife modestly,
> And if there is any honor in her,
> She will become an obedient wife . . .
> But if she remains self-willed,
> And refuses what is fair and reasonable,
> And opposes you in all requests,
> Ever disobedient and rebellious,
> On those occasions when she spurns your cooperation,
> You may punish her with blows—
> Yet do so with reason and modestly,
> So that no harm is done to either of you.
> Use both a carrot and a stick
> To bring about companionship.[6]

Here it is clear that the marriage covenant implied the right to correct or punish one's wife if such was necessary to maintain "order." As we have previously discussed, this would not have been considered violence because it would have been defined as constructive (maintaining order) rather than destructive (creating disorder). This kind of constructive violence has been understood as appropriate discipline, necessary punishment, or teaching. Through marriage one found a means of granting stability to a family system in relation to economic opportunities, inheritance, education, and social class. During the nineteenth century the Victorian family model arose as the structure that most clearly informs contemporary understandings of what a "traditional" family and marriage should be. As the nuclear family, rather than the extended family, took on greater importance in the nineteenth century, the marriage covenant became even more essential for control.

Though marriage, in our society, may have already lost its power to ensure a lifelong commitment, this ideal of eternal and unbroken love remains a powerful force in our cultural experience of marriage. This is especially true within the Roman

Catholic Church, where indissolubility remains a primary mark of the Catholic position on marriage. Annulments speak to this issue in a powerful way. In the Roman Catholic Church, one may receive only an annulment, not a divorce. An annulment is a claim that no marriage ever occurred. The impossibility of dissolving a marriage is so central to the Catholic perspective that it is more appropriate to state that the marriage was not really a marriage at all than ever to admit that a marriage could actually be dissolved.[7] The absolute and eternal aspect of this covenant is central to its character as a sacrament, which parallels the covenant between God and God's people. But it also implies a symbolic power that leads many to feel trapped in a destructive marriage.

One can also see this expectation of an eternal covenant present in the Protestant context in a study on pastors' approaches to situations of intimate violence. In the 1982 Church Response Survey, in which researchers asked clergy to respond to different scenarios, some of the questions involved scenarios of domestic violence. In one, a woman tells a minister that she has "been frequently beaten by a violent spouse, and has received numerous injuries during her nine year marriage." The pastors were asked to respond by addressing how likely they would be to recommend either separation or reunion. The results are telling of the theological underpinnings of the desire for reunion. One-third of the respondents to this study "felt that abuse would have to be severe in order to justify a Christian wife leaving her husband, while twenty-one percent felt that no amount of abuse would justify a separation. . . . Twenty-six percent of the pastors agreed that a wife should submit to her husband and trust that God would honor her action by either stopping the abuse or giving her the strength to endure it."[8]

It is hopeful that the majority of those responding did feel that there were circumstances in which separation was appropriate. At the same time, it is alarming that, only recently, nearly one out of four pastors was so convinced by the "theology of reunion" that no circumstances existed under which the covenant should be broken. This level of endorsement of abuse requires a detailed examination of the way in which reconciliation is understood as *reunion* rather than re-conciliation (rejoining the community). It is the obligation of any theology concerned with the well-being of parishioners to examine critically the theological underpinnings that allow pastors to recommend that a woman being severely abused stay with her partner and hope that an omnipotent God will come to her rescue.

Marriage is the institutional symbol that remains the central image of the covenantal relationship between the divine and humanity. In Scripture (especially Eph. 5:21-33) and theology, the bride and bridegroom are symbols used to describe the relationship between God and God's people. The Catholic rite of marriage, for example, begins "Father, you have made the union of man and woman so holy a mystery that it symbolizes the marriage of Christ and his Church."[9] The covenantal language of Christ as the bridegroom and the church as the bride also raises the patriarchal images of the ever-faithful male and the often unfaithful female. The church may stray at times, but God is always faithful to the covenant. This imagery is powerful yet dangerous. To establish males as ever faithful and women as sinful or adulterous creates a symbolic structure that further perpetuates a patronizing and demeaning attitude on the part of the husband and invites women to remain in a relationship that may be harmful and is certainly less than respectful.

Wives Be Submissive

The Southern Baptist Convention, during its 1998 general assembly, reaffirmed its commitment to a fairly literal interpretation of Eph. 5:22-23, in which the convention stated that a wife is "to submit herself graciously to the servant leadership of her husband."[10] The convention claimed that a proper hierarchy exists within the family, and God has ordained it. They argued that the love and respect called for in the rest of this passage mitigates the hierarchy established. The public outcry over the convention's stand and the ongoing debate over the meaning and authority of passages like this reflect contemporary uncertainty over the symbol of marriage.

Is there anything positive in this struggle? I believe there is. This text certainly raises the question of the relationship between men and women in marriage. It opens the discussion of power, control, and violence in relationships. Instead of pastors' attempting to avoid the issue when the passage occurs as a part of a Sunday's reading, they should use it to spark a discussion of domestic violence. The images in the biblical text call for interpretation, and it is necessary to call attention to issues of power and control in the home. I think the most appropriate response would be to focus a sermon at least once a year on domestic violence, using Col. 3:18 or another of the New Testament "household codes."

Rape in Marriage

Violence in marriage is not limited to physical assaults and verbal abuse. It also includes sexual violence. In fact many women in shelters claim that the sexual violence is far worse than the broken bones or black eyes. One means of understanding the dynamics of all marital violence is by focusing on marital rape.

In the movie *What's Love Got to Do with It?* Tina Turner tells the story of intimate violence in her own marriage. The movie unveils an abusive marital relationship based on control and fueled by a sense of inadequacy on the part of her husband. Ike Turner, her husband, is unable to accept any criticism from Tina. When the band is in financial trouble and Tina suggests he should change his style, he becomes outraged. He drags her into their private recording studio, beats her, and then brutally rapes her. The rape is chilling in its presentation.

Marital rape is a phenomenon that many men wish to avoid discussing. Men feel uncomfortable considering themselves as rapists within the marital relationship. Society itself has only recently started to convict men of date rape and marital rape, and it remains one of the most difficult crimes to prosecute successfully. Until 1977 no laws existed by which a woman could legally accuse her husband of rape.[11] Many states still place formidable obstacles to a man being charged with raping his wife.[12]

Diana Russell tells the stories of hundreds of women who have been raped and beaten by their husbands. One such case is that of Diana Green. In 1980 her unborn child died because of injuries sustained during a beating and rape by her husband, Kevin Green. He was charged with murder, rape, and assault, as described in a newspaper article:

> Green was first arrested in October after he allegedly beat and raped his wife Diana, then twenty, for refusing to have sex with him. After the alleged attack, the woman, who was nine months pregnant at the time, was rushed to the hospital in a coma. When delivered several hours later, the infant was not breathing, and attempts to resuscitate the baby failed.
>
> Because Mrs. Green was in a coma, charges against her husband were dropped and he was released from custody. Harris [the prosecuting attorney] said the woman came out of the coma about two weeks later, but her speech was impaired and she could not communicate. After three months of intensive speech therapy, investigators said they were able to piece together her story, and Green was arrested.
>
> The paper said she testified that her husband came to their Tustin bedroom and tried to force her to have sex with him even though her baby was two weeks overdue. Mrs. Green said that when she resisted her husband, he picked up a large metal key container and belted her in the forehead. She said she remembers little of what happened after that.
>
> According to the prosecution, the baby died from lack of oxygen because the placenta became detached.[13]

In light of Christianity's implicit "theology of reunion," pastors must ask, how can a religious tradition claim that reunion could be a proper response to acts such as these? Is it even possible to ask that a woman who has been brutally raped by her husband consider anything but criminal prosecution? The answer must be no. As an ecclesial community, we must be aware of the violence involved in marital rape and respond appropriately to the crime by prosecuting the offender.

The theological underpinnings of a society's denial of marital rape are significant. The lack of marital rape laws, until recently, implied societal endorsement of an "intercourse on demand" mentality within marriage. This unsaid expectation has been implied by the religious covenant and endorsed by both the society and the church. "Rape" in marriage has fallen outside of the accepted linguistic categories; thinking of rape and marriage together was impossible. Rape was considered an act of lust committed by one man on another man's wife or daughter. It was impossible for a man to rape his own wife, because there was no way of speaking about this within the symbolic and linguistic framework that existed at the time.

The historic connection between the symbols of violence and marriage has bequeathed Western societies a starkly ambiguous legacy. On the one hand, marriage has the capacity to evoke some of the highest ideals of equality, friendship, steadfastness, forgiveness, and creativity. Yet marriage also holds within itself the potential for abuse, torture, and rape. Marriage can be used to hide these crimes, and, worse still, marriage can demand that the wife return to her husband for further abuse or punishment. If she does not return, she faces guilt at having abandoned what she has regarded as a religious covenant and perhaps even admonition from the church.

The Theodicy Question

When violence occurs in an intimate relationship, a rush of questions, practical, emotional, and even metaphysical, ensues. Both the ecclesial community and each person in the violated relationship may ask many of the following questions: How do we heal the violence? Can we remain in relation? Can we find a new way of relating after violence has occurred? Why has God allowed this to happen? Historically, many theodicies have attempted to "explain" violence in terms of some higher purpose.[14] A theodicy is a theory that explains the way in which God is connected to evil. In her book *Tragic Vision and Divine Compassion*, Wendy Farley outlines four basic theodicies. Violations are understood as "punishment for sin, as elements of a larger aesthetic harmony, as purgation or pedagogy, or as presaging eschatological correction."[15] Violence, including intimate violence or marital rape, can insidiously become a part of a theological or ontological structure, a necessary piece in an unfolding universe. Many victims become doubly so when they assume that somehow, for some reason, God willed them to be hurt.

Examination of the cultural and symbolic heritage of marriage shows a need to address the "dangerous memories" the marriage carries with it. Marriage should never become a symbol or sacrament that supports, condones, or colludes with intimate violence. To avoid this possibility, the process of reconciliation, rather than marriage, must become the primary means of addressing intimate violation. By moving from a focus on marriage to a focus on reconciliation, the church advances from its historic commitment to reunion to a commitment to responsibility and healing. When reconciliation is understood properly, it can be used to supersede the symbolic call for reunion present in the symbol and sacrament of marriage. Our notions of the sacredness of marriage may need to dissolve in many cases, ironically, to make room for the genuine healing power of the divine.

Marriage as a Symbol of Hope

Although marriage has a destructive side, it remains a symbol of hope. Marriage is not only a patriarchal institution but also a place in which women can thrive and find their best selves. Marriage is thus not an inherently evil institution. Quite the opposite: given mutuality, responsibility, and accountability, marriage reveals one possibility of relationship in which to discover the clear presence of the divine. Indeed, marriages based on love and respect offer dignity and opportunities for growth to both partners. One can see this in the Equality Wheel used by the Duluth Curriculum (adapted here; see Figure 5). The equality wheel is a vision of how a relationship can be structured in opposition to the Power and Control Wheel.

Figure 5. The Equality Wheel

This wheel is used in treatment programs for batterers to show men how a relationship based on equality can replace one centered on power and control. The spokes of the wheel are behaviors that promote and carry the power of respect throughout the relationship and to the whole family. The rim of nonviolence holds the wheel together, and it is the starting point of any movement away from the dynamics of abuse we have discussed above. It is not an easy process for men to change their behaviors, but the Equality Wheel embodies an ideal for all relationships and specifies alternative behaviors. It can also offer a point of connection between nonviolent members of the church community and the batterer, as the model of respectful mutuality central to the wheel offers virtues to which everyone can aspire.

Marriage is an ambiguous symbol: it can disclose beautiful possibilities of love and exploration; it can also become a trap within which women are held captive and tortured. As marriage discloses the possibility of covenantal love, it also can be perverted into a covenant that emphasizes "for better or worse" to the point of abuse and torture. By challenging this latter possibility of marriage and calling for accountability, responsibility, and healing, reconciliation takes precedence over and corrects the distorted vision of marriage found in much of the tradition.

Images of the Divine

As we have already seen in this chapter, symbolic language is no less important to the lives of individual Christians than it is to the life of the church as a whole. No symbolic language may be more important than that used to name the divine.[16] The divine mystery that Judaism and Christianity name God, Yahweh, or *abba* is one of the most powerful symbols in the Western world. But what pertinence has imagining the divine to domestic violence? Mary Daly once said, "If God is male, the male is God."[17] The question of how we name God and the metaphors we use for God are crucial to any religious reaction to domestic violence. The classical images of God presented in most churches have come powerfully into popular religious consciousness but in ways that often distort Christian convictions about God and wreak havoc in familial relationships. The classical picture has been deeply fractured over the past generation by the new metaphors introduced in feminist, womanist, and *mujerista* theologies, as well as many other liberation theologies. A brief examination of old and new metaphors for God shows how the use of these images can help or hinder work with batterers.

God in Control

One of the central images of the historic Judeo-Christian tradition is the claim that God is sovereign of all creation. All creation depends on God. Yes, humans have free will, but God's power over the universe works through this freedom in some complex way so as to ensure both God's sovereignty and human freedom. Yet what does this claim mean in the parlance of popular U.S. Christianity? Does God "control" the world in the same way as the men discussed in chapters 1 and 2 control their families? Or, to turn it around, do men control their families based on their understanding of God's "controlling" creation? Do they see their authority as divinely derived?

God has historically been understood as omnipotent—all powerful. Today feminist and process theologians have questioned this image because it is difficult to reconcile with human freedom, divine benevolence, and the biblical portrait of a loving God. Can God love the universe if God "controls" the universe? Doesn't love require being in a relationship with another who is fully free to love in return? The image of God as lover, for example, is an important and instructive metaphor because it can be understood in a controlling or noncontrolling way. For this reason, it has the ambiguity of most deep symbols; it carries potential for both good and evil. If God is in control of creation, then God "loves" as the abusive men "love." God controls and protects the universe, guaranteeing that all will work out for the best. If on the other hand, God loves but does not control the universe, then creation is able to give the gift of love in return.

What do we lose if God is no longer in control? We certainly lose the sense of safety and security that comes with knowing that everything is in God's hands. We lose the security of knowing that no matter what we do, all will be made right by God. We lose the security of knowing that the violence and tragedy we confront in the world are all a part of a much larger plan that we do not understand. In spite of these losses, a truer and more satisfying picture—personally, interpersonally, and theologically—is to be gained. We gain a God who is vulnerable and therefore a God to whom we can relate in our own brokenness. We gain the possibility of loving God on our own, of being in a true relationship with our God. We gain the responsibility that goes along with being in a relationship, both with God and with other creatures. We gain the recognition that if God is open and responsive to our choices, we should be open and responsive to the choices of those around us.

On a more practical level for pastors and counselors, abandoning the historic preoccupation with divine sovereignty requires us to respond differently to men and women involved in domestic violence. The statement of one-third of the pastors in the Church Response Survey, that a wife "should submit to her husband and trust that God would honor her action by either stopping the abuse or giving her the strength to endure it," must be questioned, indeed repudiated. If God is no longer in control of the universe, God did not will the abuse nor see it as part of a larger plan; nor will God bypass human freedom by intervening. It is up to the church, the pastor, the community, and the friends and family of the abused woman to create an environment in which the abuse will stop. The responsibility is transferred from God to humanity. It is our responsibility to build the community of just relationships that Jesus called for in his parables and preaching, and it is through the actions of our hands, enticed and persuaded by the divine mystery, that it is accomplished.

God as Omniscient and Omnipresent

Another important historic characteristic of God is omniscience—that God knows everything—and omnipresence—that God is present at every moment to every event. God knows everything that has happened and will happen. God sees all. God is present with us at every moment of sorrow and joy. What could be wrong with these descriptions of the divine life? The danger in attributing these characteristics to God is that they continue and amplify a harmful notion of the controlling nature of God. If men head their families as God heads creation, then men must know everything and be everywhere. Men who internalize these desired characteristics use them as important means of controlling the people they claim to love. They must know everyone that their wives talked to today. They must know every aspect of every relationship they have. Men often perpetuate the illusion of omniscience by spying on their partners at work or following them when they go on errands. A man can then tell his partner that he saw her talking with the man at the checkout counter. He can also ask how much she spent on the cup of coffee she stopped to get on her way home from the store.

The church community should not valorize this stalking behavior nor the sick religious distortions that bolster it. The church instead should champion the idea that lovers build up their partners' freedom and encourage their partners to be involved in their own friendships, activities, and dreams. Knowing everything about someone invades his or her freedom and individuality. The idea that true love involves absolute and perfect knowledge is a distortion of the notion that the two shall become one. The individuality of each person in a loving relationship is essential to the ongoing growth and life of the relationship. If there is only one person in the relationship because the second person has been so confined, limited, and controlled, there is no genuine relationship.

God's Vulnerability in Christ

Two classic images of the divine in the person of Jesus are that God is vulnerable and God is self-emptying. These two metaphors may be negative or problematic images when applied to the women who have been abused by their partners, but when applied to abusive men, these characteristics are important images on which to meditate. In the person of Jesus, God becomes the one who empties Godself, who discards the images of being all powerful, all knowing, and ever present. Jesus is a man who is unable to step down from the cross, does not know why his God has abandoned him, and is limited to existing in one place at one time. He is a man who is fully present to the time and place in which he is located, and through this full presence he is able to love fully and to live in authentic relationship with those around him.

Jesus is vulnerable to the relationships in which he is involved. He suffers with the poor around him; he does not control them or magically change their condition. Jesus knows the beauty and danger of relationships. He is betrayed by one of his closest friends. Jesus calls contemporary men out of their illusion of control. He calls them to become cognizant of their own brokenness. He also calls abusive men to become accountable and responsible for their own actions and to seek forgiveness in the community established in his name.

As we complete the first part of this project, chapters 1 through 3, we have seen the phenomenon of domestic abuse, tried to fathom its dynamics through a variety of contemporary perspectives, explored its religious dimensions, and seen how some of the greatest doctrinal insights of classical Christianity have refracted in distorted and harmful ways in familial life. These primary experiences and symbols must also figure in fashioning a Christian ministry of reconciliation for abusive men. The symbol of reconciliation must be faithful to these insights if it is to be a genuine sign of God's healing presence. Reconciliation must respond to the general dynamics of violence and the specific dynamics of intimate violence. Additionally, reconciliation must transcend distortions in the cultural legacy of marriage as a sacramental and symbolic aspect of Western Christianity. Marriage, when it is understood as a symbol of a never-ending relationship, even when it involves physical or sexual abuse, is a distorted and oppressive symbol. The analysis of violence and marriage also discloses the difficulty of proposing an adequate and truly healing understanding of reconciliation. The Christian tradition has supported violation in subtle yet systematic ways by misunderstanding the depth of violation present. The church often gives simplistic responses to violations, which merely continue the violation of women and children. It will be the goal of the second part of this project to sketch a vision of Christian reconciliation that maintains the desire to heal violation without the insidious tendency to condone or support violation.

4

Reconciliation: A Model for Addressing Male Violence

Such was the wickedness in which I agonized, blaming myself more sharply than ever, turning and twisting in my chain as I strove to tear free from it completely, for slender indeed was the bond that still held me. . . . I shrank from dying to death and living to life, for ingrained evil was more powerful in me than new grafted good. The nearer it came, that moment when I would be changed, the more it pierced me with terror. Dismayed, but not quite dislodged, I was left hanging.

AUGUSTINE OF HIPPO

In *Deep Symbols: Their Postmodern Effacement and Reclamation,* Edward Farley argues that the deep symbols of the Christian tradition have lost their power in the postmodern context but that there is a means of reclaiming them.[1] Farley claims that these deep symbols must be purged of their false accretions from each historical period. But more than mere purgation is necessary, he argues. We must also "find ways to remember the mystery and give it expression in the face of what appear to be overwhelming discreditations and displacements."[2] Farley highlights tradition, obligation, reality, law, and hope as deep symbols, and he explores how each can be reinvigorated. He explains that to reclaim an atrophied deep symbol, one must purge the layers of history that hide the power these symbols have to enchant us and to "summon the community out of its corrupted present."[3] This project attempts to augment and apply Farley's insight by addressing another of the deep symbols of the Christian tradition, reconciliation, as it relates to violent men.

So how are we to reclaim the deep symbol of reconciliation? We must first examine what enchants and awakens us, the core message of the symbol, by peeling away the false layers that have been attached to this symbol. What lies at the core of reconciliation is nothing less than the enchanting and overwhelming notion that even when a human has become so distorted and disfigured by egoism, rage, despair, and fear, that person will be embraced by the Christian community. The Christian community has within its treasure trove of symbols a call for reconciliation. We are called as Christians not to demonize those who act in evil ways but rather to call them to accountability and to love them. This requires that we ferret out the true insights in this message of hope. To do so we must turn to the history of the term *reconciliation,* as well as the history of its practice. Three short forays and one longer exploration are required if we are to understand this deep symbol. The first is to first-century Palestine, where we examine an image of the rabbi Jesus and his followers discussing the difficulty of addressing violation within their community. Second, we look to towns in Italy, Sicily, and the rest of the Mediterranean to see how, during the first five centuries, Christians developed the Order of Penitents and the Mediterranean rite of reconciliation. A third site of reconciliation is the Irish isle, where the monks who followed St. Patrick developed the Irish rite of reconciliation. These three limited encounters with the history of the symbol will be followed by a more extensive examination of Thomas Aquinas and his notion of the four essential moments to the deep symbol of reconciliation. Together these four moments will allow us to reclaim the symbol for our own time. The deep symbol of reconciliation will then be able to come to life in the parishes and communities of this century with new promise and hope. Even in nonsacramental traditions, reconciliation, properly understood, is a symbol of great depth and power that allows us to offer a liberative praxis to both the perpetrators and victims of domestic violence. So let our journey begin.

The Biblical Logic of Reconciliation

The biblical logic of reconciliation—relation, violence, and reunion—has informed the Judeo-Christian tradition's primary response to violation. It is also present in the christological theories of atonement and satisfaction.[4] When violence does occur in a relationship, we tend as Christians to understand it through this same paradigm, whether it be specified as sin or as a form of punishment, purgation, or pedagogy. The violence is still seen as only an event on the way toward reunion. Reunion is always seen as necessary for the violence to "make sense." Recently, the paradigm of reunion after violence has been questioned.[5] It has become increasingly difficult for theologians, when faced with child molestation, marital rape, rape used as a form of ethnic cleansing, or genocidal killings like those of Nazi Germany, Rwanda, or Bosnia, to continue to propose reunion as the only logical and only "Christian" response to radical evil.[6] Their chief reservation stems from an inability to accept as authentic the monolithic structure of a teleological world directed by an omnipotent God toward a perfect future.[7]

When one examines intimate violence as it actually presents itself, one finds that reunion of the violated and the violator is not always an appropriate response. The desire for reunion discussed in chapter 3 is partly the consequence of a mythic view of reconciliation as reunion. This ideal of reunion has also been placed on the relationship of intimate partners and has become a model, at times even a "Christian expectation," that after violence one "should" try to reunite with one's abuser.[8] As the church (bride) and Christ (bridegroom) have been able to reunite, so the survivor (bride) and the perpetrator (bridegroom) should also be able to reunite. This view does not take seriously the dynamics of intimate violence and does not take into account the physical and psychological scarring that has occurred. Reconciliation should not be confused with nor conflated into reunion.

Reconciliation in the Early Christian Tradition

The beginnings of a theology of reconciliation lie in the Jewish tradition. Judaism understands itself as a community of faith bound by a covenant. The covenant between God and God's people is permeated with acts of forgiveness and reconciliation. The issues of forgiveness and reconciliation are central to the ministry and communities that followed after the rabbi Jesus. One finds many stories and parables addressing the issue of forgiveness in the teachings of Jesus. The prodigal son, the woman at the well, and the stoning of Mary all focus on the nature of forgiveness in the reign of God professed by Jesus.[9] When Peter asked how many times he must forgive, he was amazed by the reply of seventy times seven times. The proposal of seven made by Peter far exceeded the accepted Jewish custom. According to Matt. 18:22, there is no limit to forgiveness within the community of Jesus. At the same time, the Gospels evince a clear denunciation of oppression at every level. Judgment is a reality within Jesus' ministry, but it is a judgment of the powerful and the religious elite. The balance between justice and forgiveness remains central to Christian theology throughout its struggle to embrace the truths revealed in the life and ministry of Jesus.

The early Christian communities codified Jesus' teachings on forgiveness and judgment. These passages became the foundational texts out of which Tertullian, Augustine, Thomas Aquinas, and Martin Luther formulated their specific visions of reconciliation. The early Christian church desired to maintain certain boundaries as beyond repentance. This emphasis on judgment was always tempered by Jesus' words, "Stop judging, that you may not be judged" (Matt. 7:1). The tension between justice and forgiveness created one of the early puzzles for Christian theologians and the church itself.

Two major developments move us from the early Christian communities in Palestine to contemporary forms of reconciliation in the churches. Amid the many changes and fluctuations in the understandings and implementation of reconciliation over two thousand years, two basic structures stand out. The first is the Mediterranean practice of penance in the Christian communities of the Roman Empire during the first six centuries. The second is the introduction of the Irish Penitential books in the fifth century and their eventual monopolization of the Rite of Penance through the Middle Ages and into the Reformation and Counter-Reformation.

During the first five centuries of Christianity in and around the Mediterranean center of Rome, the penitential rite developed as a communal public display of remorse or contrition and acceptance of the responsibility connected to sin. For example, in the Order of Penitents, created in the third century and continued as a part of the church's tradition until the Irish rite squeezed it out by the end of the twelfth century, the bishops chose the members, who were "sinners" selected to participate in public forms of penance. Members of the Order of Penitents remained so for life. Substantial penalties went along with one's entrance into this order.[10] The severity of the penance, which included public humiliation and often beatings, made it clear that this was to be an order for only a select few. Although everyone within the Christian community sinned, only a few individuals involved in the most grievous cases were forced by a bishop into the Order of Penitents. Three characteristics of the Mediterranean rite of reconciliation thus define it: public confession, permanent status of being a penitent, and lengthy exclusion from communal celebration.

The Irish Penitential Books, which developed as a direct result of the isolation the Irish monks felt on this island of "infidels" a week's journey from Rome, exhibit significant changes from the Mediterranean rite as well as some problematic new ideas. Saint Patrick traveled to Ireland in the fifth century and established monastic communities among the druids who lived on the island at the time. Three characteristics of the Celtic rite of penance have been identified by Hugh Connelly that seem especially relevant to our study.[11] First, penance had no public character. The Order of Penitents did not exist in Ireland, nor was there a sense of public accountability or shame. Instead, the penitent performed a series of private exercises that usually involved fasting and prayer. Second, the reconciliation or healing was also private rather than public. Reconciliation was granted in private, after all or a portion of the requisite exercises had been achieved. Third, confession was to occur on a regular basis, that is, the rite was understood as repeatable.

If the contemporary church is to learn from the historical wanderings of those who have struggled with the reality of violation and the persistent desire for forgiveness and reunion, it must recognize the strengths and weaknesses of both the Mediterranean and the Celtic rites. As a means of responding to the enduring and cyclical character of intimate violence, reconciliation should side with the Mediterranean claim that certain actions call for an Order of Penitents, meaning a group that develops a sustained program of reconciliation. The ecclesial community can also recognize with the Celtic rite that reconciliation is repeatable. The idea present in the Mediterranean model that one had only one chance and then one was permanently banished from the community is not appropriate in responding to intimate violence.

What is absent from the history of reconciliation is an analysis of the layers of healing that are required in authentic reconciliation. Both models of the early church are primarily individualistic. The proposal presented in this chapter develops the insights of the classical tradition of reconciliation as part of a multidimensional approach.

A Thomistic Interpretation of Reconciliation

Reconciliation found its classical formulation in the thirteenth century in the sacramental theology of Thomas Aquinas. Aquinas identified four distinct, though interconnected, moments in the sacrament of reconciliation: contrition, confession, satisfaction, and absolution.[12] We will examine each in turn. These four moments embody a kind of phenomenology of the healing desired in reconciliation, each moment revealing a specific requisite dimension of healing. Using Thomas's framework, we are able to establish a connection to the historical articulations of the deep symbol of reconciliation while at the same time answering the contemporary demands of social scientific conclusions about intimate violence. Aquinas's scheme acts as the synthesizing element in this work. Through his four aspects of reconciliation the practice has the capacity to regain its genuine character as a classic symbol of Christianity. These four characteristics flow one from the other, and together they form a series of events that enable healing for the penitent and safety for the survivors and the community. The desire to confront violation in its totality and see that healing occurs for the perpetrator, survivors, and the ecclesial community is central to the initial formulation of an effective contemporary form of reconciliation.

Contrition

Three elements contribute to a definition of contrition: grief, detestation, and intention.[13] Grief of the soul is Thomas's way of describing the sense of compassion one can feel for one's victim and the sorrow associated with the violation of the other. Compassion and sorrow are only possible when one recognizes the victim as truly other and vulnerable. The grief one feels when one recognizes that one has violated the other is the beginning stage of contrition. The detestation of the sin involves a felt disgust with the violation itself. Detestation of the acts committed might or might not be present initially in many of those who are violating their partners. If the penitent is to have a contrite heart, the penitent must feel the pain and violation of the other. One sign that contrition is present is when the perpetrator hates the act of violation itself. By intending not to violate the other in the future, one makes a commitment to change and a commitment to self-enhancement and growth (*metanoia*).

Significantly, Aquinas distinguishes between imperfect and perfect contrition. A sense of contrition brought about by a desire to avoid guilt or punishment (*attritio*) differs vastly from contrition brought about by love of God (*contritio*). The former is motivated by fear. Even though *attritio* was imperfect, scholastics deemed it acceptable for the sacrament of penance.[14] Perfect contrition *(contritio)*, motivated out of a perfect love for God, is able to bring about a truly penitent heart. Love of God that is motivated by selfish desire, even the desire to avoid sin so as to avoid punishment and guilt, is not sufficient for perfect contrition. The distinction between *contritio* and *attritio* is primarily a distinction between motivations: fear and love. One finds that most men, court-ordered into a batterers' treatment program, experience *attritio* rather than *contritio* as they move through the work of accountability. It is the goal of the ecclesial community to lead violent men to a true sense of contrition. It is also important that the ecclesial community not be fooled into thinking that a batterers' attitude of attrition is actually the sign of a contrite heart.

Aquinas tellingly notes that contrition involves crushing the hard will. An example of the hardness and rigidity of the will is the emotional shield that abusive men build around themselves. A batterer may feel internal pain, but he has learned that he cannot expose himself to the world, because the potential for further pain would be too great. He is unable to be intimate with anyone, because it would involve too great a risk. The typical batterer is no longer willing to expose himself to any pain or embarrassment, and so he becomes hardened.

James Gilligan explains the results of this hardening in terms of an emotional deadening of the self:

> When emotional pain is overwhelming, it provokes an automatic, unconscious, reflex like self-anesthetization, a self-deadening. . . . The kind of man I am describing protects himself from the emotional suffocation of living in a loveless atmosphere by withdrawing the love he has begun to feel from everyone and everything, in an attempt to reserve for himself whatever capacity for love he may have. . . . But his withdrawal of love from everyone and everything around him not only protects him from emotional pain, it also condemns him to the absence of emotional pleasure or joy; for we cannot enjoy the people who make up our world, cannot enjoy being with them, except to the degree that we love

them. So the person who cannot love cannot have any feelings—
pain or joy.[15]

The deadening of the soul, seen here in research with violent
prison inmates, is like the hardening of the will proposed by
Aquinas. Is it possible for someone who can feel nothing to feel
guilt? There is no possibility of contrition until this shell is broken down. This breaking of the hard will requires a certain
amount of love to be given to these men. It is not punishment that
will allow for reconciliation; the ecclesial response must be one of
love, a love that recognizes their violence but offers each individual an opportunity to exist in a relationship that is not painful but
accepting and nurturing. As Gilligan says,

> If the current environment [prison] were actually more humane,
> it would at least be a bit easier for many of these men to recog-
> nize that the source of their most intolerable distress [the
> absence of feeling] is not their present environment, bad as that
> is, but in themselves; i.e., in their memories of past experiences,
> and in the means by which they attempt and are still attempting
> to protect themselves from the pain of those experiences and
> their memories. This is one reason why a humane environment is
> an absolute prerequisite for the healing of violent men, and why
> punitive environments only perpetuate the violence of criminals
> who are placed in them.[16]

Aquinas claims that *contrition* comes from the phrase "to crush
something," to crush the will into little pieces so that one can
begin to see the love of God. This is also necessary in the cases of
the most violent men in our society. It is necessary to break down
the wall that has been built to avoid pain. Only after this barrier
is deconstructed will the violent man be able to recognize the
humanity of the other.

Contrition is a difficult and often illusory aim. Feeling contrite
may merely lead to shallow confession and meaningless short-
lived acts of kindness that do not complete reconciliation or heal
the wounds caused by violation. The stage of "loving contrition"
exhibited by many violent abusers is a mockery of genuine recon-

ciliation. That kind of "loving contrition," as we have already seen in the discussion of the third stage of Lenore Walker's cycle of violence (see Figure 1, chapter 1), is counterproductive. It is dangerous because it masks the continued desire for control.[17] An abusive man often feels some sorrow after he has beaten his wife. He states that it will never happen again, he confesses his undying love, and he brings flowers to the hospital room.

Lenore Walker explains the lengths to which this "loving contrition" can be taken when she describes visiting a battered woman in the hospital. Alice was brought to the emergency room after being beaten so badly that she lost one of her kidneys and almost died on the operating table. Lenore Walker describes what she saw when she came to visit Alice two days after the beating:

> When I got off the elevator the next day, the flowers had reached the nurses' station. This time when I walked into the room, Alice was sitting up. It was hard to believe that this was the same woman who had been so defeated and injured only two days earlier. She was bubbly and excited. She told me how delighted she was that she and Mike were going off on a wonderful cruise as soon as she got out of the hospital.[18]

The men who come to hospital rooms across the country and state how sorry they are and that it will never happen again are also the men who claim in court or in group that they never beat her, instead offering such excuses as, "She slipped and fell against the stove." Minimizing, denying, and blaming are used by these men to avoid contrition and confession. They are sometimes sorry when faced with the immediacy of their partner's wounds. But when confronted with the long-lasting and difficult road of *metanoia* necessitated by batterers' treatment programs, they pull their defensive armor back on and stand against the rest of the world, righteous in their own eyes.

Authentic contrition, according to Aquinas, is an ongoing integral part of the sacramental process of reconciliation. One's whole life must be lived with a contrite heart. Aquinas's words remain powerful today, when read in the context of the cycle of violence:

"It seems that one ought to always grieve for one's sins. . . . *The time for contrition is the whole of the present state of life.* For as long as one is a wayfarer, one detests the obstacles that retard or hinder one from reaching the end of the way."[19]

To summarize Aquinas's definition of contrition, it entails a hatred of the violation itself, a love of God that precludes the violation of the other, the breaking of the self-centered will, and never-ending sorrow about the violation. These characteristics of *contritio* lead directly to the second aspect of reconciliation, the act of confession.

Confession

We can see here the benefits of the proposal that reconciliation be communal and not individual and that contrition itself is not enough. Authentic reconciliation requires a communal expression of contrition and a communal confession. It also involves satisfaction appropriate to the nature of the violation. Without all three of these steps, there is little hope for responsibility on the part of the violator, and little hope of "absolution." Without a group or community to which the man can be held accountable, the sorrow of contrition will soon transform into indignation, anger, desire for control, and further abuse.

In a relational ecclesiology, confession can be re-understood as an ongoing process of accountability. For example, the ecclesial community might offer a group setting in which men who have been violent would have an opportunity to confess their violent acts. These groups could be established as a batterers' treatment program or as a church group that runs parallel and remains in contact with the community's treatment program for batterers. "Confession" within this group, which is usually referred to as "check-in" in batterers' treatment programs, would allow the members of the group to encourage the batterer as he moves toward the stage of satisfaction. In most batterers' treatment groups, check-in is used as a means of maintaining accountability among the men. (An example of a weekly check-in log can be seen in Appendix 3.) This group can also provide greater safety for the victims of violence through a better understanding of the crime that occurred. Because the group is devoted to the well-being of the penitent, it would not allow the penitent to be exposed to public humiliation and shame.

This form of group confession is an attempt to minimize abuses associated with the Celtic and Mediterranean models of confession. The Celtic rite was abusive in that it focused exclusively on individual confession and therefore tended toward a lack of accountability. The Mediterranean rite overemphasized public confession, using it as a means of humiliating and sometimes torturing those who belonged to the Order of Penitents. The desire for public and communal confession was also perverted in the Inquisition, as well as during the witch-hunts of the eighteenth century.

A continuation of this perverted public confession is present in contemporary society, particularly among many public religious figures. Jim and Tammy Faye Baker, Jimmy Swaggart, and politicians Marion Barry, Newt Gingrich, Bill Clinton, and Jesse Jackson have used very public confessions as a means of avoiding the enduring work of contrition and escaping from the responsibility inherent in satisfaction. By doing so, they continue their political and religious careers seemingly unscathed. This trend is unhealthy and unhelpful in that it lacks the connection to contrition, satisfaction, and absolution. Confession on its own, devoid of *contritio* and acts of satisfaction, becomes no more than a public relations gimmick. Detecting the hypocrisy involved in many of these public confessions, one can see that, if community-based confession is necessary, then it must be more than merely shouting one's sins to as many people as will listen. Confessions that spread through the mass media cannot be considered an appropriate confession to a community.

For confession to hold true to the insights of both the Mediterranean and the Celtic rite, it must focus on both community and responsibility. The central insight of the Mediterranean rite is that public confession within the context of a caring community is central to reconciliation. The Celtic rite implies that any confession must involve also a personal relationship with someone who cares about the penitent's well-being and will hold him or her responsible. To blend these two insights together, the contemporary church must focus on communal responsibility within a small group of people who truly care about the well-being of the penitent. This group is to be in solidarity with the rest of the community and so will hold the penitent accountable. The community of responsibility must be willing to share in the responsibility of the penitent to make amends and also be willing to walk the road of conversion with the penitent.

Confession put in terms of sharing one's story should always be an integral part of a batterer's treatment. Being honest and accountable appears to be one of the first steps in accepting the violation one has perpetrated. Similarly, the church community's practice of reconciliation, whether sacramentally expressed or not, must begin to focus on an intimate community of reconciliation within the larger church community. This small group would be willing to hold the penitents responsible while at the same time calling them to conversion and full unity with the larger church community. This call to conversion must be focused on love and respect, not vengeance and disgust. After the penitent has confessed his or her failings to the group, the facilitators of the group and the group members can call the penitent to acts of satisfaction as a further step on the road of conversion and healing.

Satisfaction

The third element of reconciliation, according to Aquinas, is satisfaction. Aquinas's definition of satisfaction demands that the actions taken by the penitent satisfy the debt or heal the wound caused by her or his sin. This sense of wounding or disease is threefold: (1) the wounding of the victim, (2) the wounding of the church and God, and (3) the wounding of the penitent. It is clear in the cases we have cited above that women beaten by men have had their whole person—body, psyche, and spirit—wounded and often scarred by the violation. God and the community of the church have been violated by the rupture in the deep relationality of God and humanity and the harm that violence does to the trust and amity that underwrite community. The person who has committed the violence has also been wounded.

If reconciliation as a whole is to be a healing process, one that works toward the gradual salvation of both survivor and perpetrator, then the ecclesial community must take into account the nature of the violation. The church must understand the nature of violation, not for the sake of punishment and humiliation, as we see in the examples of the Order of Penitents and the torturing of "infidels" during the Inquisition and the New England witch trials. Rather, the ecclesial community should demonstrate through satisfaction its desire to see that the perpetrator be held responsible for the violation as a necessary means to his own healing and the healing of his victims. The offenses of intimate violence should be met with a desire to satisfy the wrongs and attempt to heal the wounds. This requires that the ecclesial community understand the reality of the injuries. Satisfaction must first focus on the healing and care of the victims. Second, satisfaction must focus on the need for the perpetrator to learn how to connect intimately to others. The community can come to know whether the confession is genuine by whether the batterer is being fully accountable for his behavior. For a complete analysis of how to recognize that a batterer is being accountable, see Appendix 2.

Is the role of our community to mete out forgiveness and punishment, or is it to help people rejoin a broken community? I believe that it is the latter to which reconciliation, as a classic Christian symbol, calls the church.

Absolution

Addressing the possibility of absolution, we must never forget the call for never-ending responsibility. Aquinas discusses absolution in terms of the remission of guilt. He understood the goal of penance to be healing, the removal of mortal sin. Mortal sin was the deadliest of offenses because it involved turning away from God in such a severe way as to deserve eternal damnation. God's grace was present to the church through the sacraments. If one's sins were absolved, one no longer deserved the eternal punishment of damnation. Absolution did not mean that one could forget about the violation, or that one had relinquished all responsibility for satisfaction of the debt owed. This position is seen in Aquinas's description of absolution from the *Summa contra Gentiles:* "Though guilt is taken away and the debt of eternal punishment is canceled, there still remains some obligation to the temporal punishment, to save the justice of God, which redresses fault by punishment."[20] Though Aquinas calls on the violation-punishment model of the Hebrew Scriptures present in this passage, he also addresses the relative character of the term *absolution*. Absolution does not mean that the church denies the existence of a previously committed sin.[21] The church is disclosing to the penitent the reality of God's abundant mercy. God loves the penitent in spite of his or her sin. The church passes the mystery of this love on to the penitent through absolution. Yet this love, which embraces the penitent for eternity, requires that the penitent live a life of ongoing conversion. Absolution is not a clean slate but an assurance of the love of God in the midst of brokenness.

Absolution has been understood as the end or goal of the process of reconciliation since before the time of Aquinas. To be absolved of guilt by God was the goal, so that, once again, one would be able to enter heaven upon one's death. This view of absolution has several specific theological problems that cannot be adequately addressed in this brief text. Without resolving the issues, we can raise certain important starting points for revising the traditional notion.

First, absolution has implied an end to the process of reconciliation. This should be dismissed on theological grounds, since Aquinas himself argued that contrition is a lifelong process. It should also be dismissed by virtue of social-scientific research that clearly demonstrates that there is no absolute cure to violent behaviors.[22] Finally absolution, understood as a simple removal of the violation, should be dismissed because it runs counter to the need for constant vigilance and responsibility.

Second, traditional absolution is often linked to soteriological beliefs that minimize the importance of the present. The issue of duration is central to any proper understanding of reconciliation. Reconciliation is a matter of being in right relation with the ecclesial community and with God. This is an issue of the present. When people become overly concerned about the future of their soul, they focus solely on their status and prospects for eternity. This mindset overemphasizes the future and so minimizes the need for ongoing conversion throughout one's life.

Third, absolution has often been understood individualistically. Absolution from guilt is far more complex when addressed within a relational theology. The depth of the ruptured relationship often implies that the relationship cannot be fully healed. Being centered within a complex of relationships means that a person is not fully healed as long as his children, wife or partner, parents, friends, neighbors, and co-workers still suffer from the violation that occurred. Absolution is a communal, not simply an individual, process that occurs over time. In a relational universe, absolution that attempts to forget about the past is irresponsible.

Clearly the human community, in its Christian expression, has recognized the need to account for violation and to heal the wounds inflicted on oneself, one's victim, and one's community. The classic symbols of Christianity work to heal the harm and repair the damage caused by the violation. Reconciliation that is solely individualistic is neither helpful nor appropriate in light of all the persons affected by violence. This individualistic approach, a legacy of the Celtic rite, has been rejected in most recent theological appropriations of reconciliation. Reconciliation must live out its linguistic roots and remain re-conciliation. Reconciliation is the re-joining of the penitent member to the rest of the community.

Reconciliation becomes false and perverted when its primary focus and goal becomes reunification, rest, or release from responsibility for one's past. The most dangerous legacy of the Christian understanding of reconciliation is the desire to have reconciliation become a matter of "forgive and forget."

Contemporary reconciliation should maintain the fourfold structure reviewed above: contrition, confession, satisfaction, and absolution. This form addresses the issues of duration, accountability, responsibility, and community. The insights gleaned from Aquinas are foundational points for reconstructing an appropriate and responsible theology of reconciliation. These insights offer us a glimpse at how this deep symbol of the Christian tradition enchants us. The hope and responsibility that come with reconciliation profoundly alter the response one has to the batterer within the church community. When James (see chapter 1) is a friend or a member of our worshipping community, it is difficult simply to dismiss and demonize him. Reconciliation offers an alternative to demonizing James. This deep symbol calls us to join him in the difficult journey of developing a contrite heart, confessing in an accountable manner, and responsibly compensating, as far as possible, for the destruction caused by his battering. As the Christian community stands with the batterers in this process, it incarnates the symbol of reconciliation and offers a glimpse of the abundant grace the church claims as its central message. The final chapter will present a responsible theology of the practical possibilities of a multidimensional approach to healing the wounds of intimate violence.

5

Reconciliation:
A Responsible Approach to Intimate Violence

Even love must pass through loneliness,
the husbandman becomes again
the Lone Hunter, and sets out
not to the familiar woods of home
but to the forest of the night,
the true wilderness, where renewal
is found, the lay of the ground
a premonition of the unknown.
Blowing leaf and flying wren
lead him on. He can no longer be at home,
he cannot return, unless he begins
the circle that first will carry him away.

WENDELL BERRY

Our probe of the cultural and religious import of intimate violence
has led to reformulating classic Christian symbols—God, salvation,
covenant, community—and especially the Christian ideal and
practice of reconciliation. Reconciliation, understood as "cheap
grace" or "forgive and forget," continues to have negative effects
on families who experience the destructiveness of intimate violence. Members of affected families often hear in the church's sug-
gestion of reconciliation a call for reunion. Women often feel that
they have failed or sinned if they do not attempt to reunite with
their abusive ex-partner. Pastors often strive to save a marriage at
great risk to the abused partner. In contrast to this understanding
of reconciliation, the ecclesial community must reclaim the root
experience of reconciliation. It does not demand reunion but
strives for healing all people involved. The ecclesial community

must recover the deep symbol of reconciliation that simultaneously emphasizes loving acceptance and demanding responsibility.

Reconciliation, in situations of intimate violence, invites the perpetrator, the survivor, and the community to greater and fuller life through the healing of wounded relationships. The violator is welcomed into the community after he has been through the process of contrition, confession, and satisfaction. The victim/survivor is welcomed into a supportive community and is not told that she must reunite with her ex-partner but, rather, is invited to join a community of compassion, advocacy, and protection.

The Christian practice of reconciliation, whether sacramentally understood or not, if it is to take seriously the nature of violation, relationality, and healing, must be multidimensional. Reconciliation must address healing in the individual sphere, the interhuman sphere, and the social sphere. Reconciliation must attempt to heal the internal brokenness of the perpetrator, allowing him to realize his own capacity to be loved by God, by others, and by himself. Healing in the interhuman sphere involves the perpetrator's relinquishing his desire to control or punish his partner and possibly his partner's capacity to forgive him. Yet, reconciliation, if it is to address the violation within the interhuman sphere, must also address the anger and resentment of the survivor of violence. To heal this resentment does not involve forgetting the violation, but creating the conditions for the survivor's being able to wish the well-being of the penitent batterer. Finally, reconciliation must heal the social relationships within the ecclesial community and the larger society. By providing an example of compassionate, responsible healing, the ecclesial community offers an alternative to vengeance. Vengeance, as René Girard has claimed, creates a never-ending spiral of violation that destroys rather than rebuilds and harms rather than heals the community. Reconciliation is a sacred process and symbol of healing. To remain a living symbol of hope, it must heal on all three levels of human relationality.

Scarring: An Important Metaphor
for Understanding Violence

As a means of further understanding this healing, we can look to the human body and its attempts to heal as an analogy to the way relationships heal after violation. When the physical body is wounded, the body immediately begins to heal itself. It engages the immune system and begins to rebuild the damaged tissue. The seriousness of the wound determines whether the body can fully replace the tissue with the same type of tissue or whether it will replace the lost tissue with another type of tissue. Our bodies respond to damage and irritation in different ways.

Three unique responses of the body are important to our analysis of violation. When we scrape ourselves and take the first couple of layers of skin off, our bodies will replace the lost tissue with identical tissue that will look and function the same as the lost tissue did. A second way in which the body heals is in specific response to constant irritation without loss of tissue. As regular irritation to the skin continues over long periods of time, the body replaces the original tissue with callous tissue, which protects the nerve endings from feeling. Callous tissue is a much tougher tissue, less likely to tear or to be irritated in the future. Finally, if the wound is very deep and not only rips through the first two layers of skin but tears away the skin deep into the flesh, the body will respond by replacing the lost tissue with scar tissue. Scar tissue has different properties than does normal epidural tissue. Scar tissue is more rigid and less flexible; it is stronger and tears less easily. These differences can be seen and felt.

These three bodily responses have relational parallels that can be recognized and heeded. In any relationship of intimacy, many small violations occur every day: we degrade the other, ignore the other, make biting or sarcastic comments, lie to our partner, or manipulate him or her for our own self-interest. These behaviors can be severe and deep violations, but normally they function much like a scrape, which hurts for a moment but over time heals. The relationship, like our skin, returns to its original state, in which each person has the capacity to love and cherish the other and to be open and flexible. If the irritating minor violations above are regularly repeated, however, one becomes callous. Constant degradation leads to a callousness within the relationship so that one can no longer feel anything—any pain, any love, or any guilt. Dead to feeling, one is willing to hurt others in order to feel something, anything. This also occurs in intimate relationships, in which the partner who is demeaned or ignored becomes callous and begins to lose his or her capacity to appreciate or be open to the one he or she claims to love.

A third response is scarring. When violence occurs in a relationship, a wound is opened that cannot be healed in the same way as one caused by a sarcastic comment or snide remark. It is possible that the healed relationship will not bear reunion but only separation. The scar will never "heal" in the sense of disappearing. In this regard, we believe that violence and severe violations scar relationships to such an extent that any reunion will always carry with it the memory of violence. As the body changes its approach to wounds when they reach a certain depth, so too must the interpersonal process of healing and reconciliation respond differently to varying degrees of violation.

Being able to accept the scar is something that must still be addressed after the wound has healed. In our model, this can be seen as the time it takes for contrition, confession, and satisfaction. The wound must be acknowledged, cleaned, and allowed time to heal. It must not be strained. Just as a deep wound on a joint, if stretched or bent, can break its stitches and cause further scarring, so too in relationships of violation. Time is necessary to allow for healing, time in which the survivor is isolated from the perpetrator. Healing often takes months or years, years in which the desire for reunion is often strong. It is only through the support of a community of responsibility and hope that one can move through the long and difficult process of reconciliation without despair.

This sense of the ongoing nature of the call to responsibility is not in keeping with the desire for reconciliation understood as reunion. The batterer grows tired of the unending demands placed on him. If only the rupture would be healed and the scar taken away, these men would feel some relief from the burden of their abusive behavior. As men in treatment groups have often said: "If only she were no longer afraid of me," or "If only my children would not leave the room every time I walked in." Alternatively stated, men ask, "When will she stop bringing up the past?" or "When will I be able to go back to a normal life?" or "When will I no longer feel guilty?" These men believe they have a right to sleep easily at night, and that their responsibility to the survivor of their violence is too much to bear. They are unwilling to accept that the memories which haunt their victims may linger for years. It is here that the community of faith and hope must stand vigilant with its message of hope for both the survivor and the perpetrator, but never as a community that neglects the safety of its members or takes the easy way out.

Healing the Individual: Reconciliation in the Individual Sphere

Violent men batter women "because they can." This statement from Richard Gelles and Murray Straus reminds us of the responsibility the community has to hold violent men accountable for their actions. At the same time we should not forget James Gilligan's claim that dehumanizing violent offenders is likely to make them more, not less, violent. Responding to violent men is not a matter of strict punishment or reminding them of their sinfulness. Instead the community must find ways of helping the violator to view himself as worthy of love, as respected and cherished by a community. This response is couched within a primary understanding of the potential danger of these men. Therefore, any group that works with violent offenders must see as its primary task advocacy for the safety and well-being of the women and children who have been violated and who are likely to be further victimized if they are not separated and shielded from the "penitent."[1] These groups should always include at least one woman co-facilitator, who understands the dynamics of intimate violence and can hold the men accountable, confronting the men when they begin to blame their victims for their own violence. This model is present in the Duluth curriculum, cited in chapter 2.

In some respects, this group would be similar to the Order of Penitents. It must recognize the nature and severity of the violation that has occurred. It consistently reminds the penitent that he must be held responsible for his violence. Unlike the Order of Penitents, however, public humiliation need not be a part of the process of reconciliation. This new "Order of Penitent Batterers" is not a group that stands at the door of the church each week begging for forgiveness. It is rather a group that meets the needs of safety within the community by embracing those who have violated an individual or individuals and the community. Expressing concern and care for violent men is the first step toward their re-entry into the community. The men must feel loved and accepted as people before they can begin to let go of their need to control others.

Am I proposing that the church take on the role of the social service agency in providing batterers' treatment for the whole community? If there is no other organization able to do this work, church communities should join together and establish programs for batterers. The most productive strategy is for churches to work together with other social service providers to support the existing batterer's treatment program. I believe that every community should recognize the importance of reconciling the violent offenders in its midst to the larger community, but this goal is only possible with an extended and rigorous program of responsibility. Where there is already a batterers' treatment program working within the community, the ecclesial community should be sure that part of the process of satisfaction involves attending these meetings.

Healing individual batterers is a process that involves the four aspects of traditional reconciliation: contrition, confession, satisfaction, and absolution. These four moments should occur within the context of a community of responsibility and support. We now turn to a brief description of how these four moments may be integrated theologically and communally in light of the first four chapters.

Contrition: The Recognition of the Face

The most significant aspect of the individual's healing process is learning the ability to recognize the other as other—that is, to be able to see one's partner as a person with her own dreams, goals, likes, dislikes, and friends. She is not a mere extension of my ego, but an "other," a person separate and different from me. When this happens, the potential for contrition becomes real, and the process of genuine reconciliation can truly begin.

Reconciliation calls each person in the ecclesial community to responsibility. Each individual helps to create a space in which healing is possible. But ultimately contrition begins with the self. It is not a communal endeavor but rather is a defining moment of the person as person. One must be able to state, "I hit my partner, and I take responsibility for my actions." Nor is feeling sorry enough. Saying one is sorry does not mean that one can now return to one's normal life. Though often men want simply to go back home and begin again, their desire comes out of the false stage of "loving contrition" and not as a sentiment of genuine contrition, which has more to do with open-eyed acknowledgment and accountability.

Confession, Satisfaction, and Absolution

Once one has felt the sorrow of genuine contrition and begins to see one's partner as a unique individual, one needs to make this stance public. As a means of remaining responsible, it is important to tell other people that one has been violent. Through confessing, one may come to realize that in spite of the horror of violation, one is still loved. Confession acts as a "reality check." By confessing to one's peers, one may see the subtlety of one's denial of responsibility.

Confession is an ongoing aspect of the life of the Order of Penitents. It is not a one-time confession. In James's story from chapter 1, it was shown that confession is a slow process of peeling back the layers of self-deception and self-protection. Like the skin on an onion, the layers of minimizing, denying, and blaming must be peeled away. Each meeting of a batterers' group involves the possibility for deeper insight into the nature of the abuse. This ongoing confession is a journey of discovery for the penitent batterer. Without a community of responsibility and love, this process is almost impossible.

The group's role as confessor demands a difficult balance between being supportive and holding the batterer accountable. Martin Buber addresses the core ethical imperative to view even the most violent offenders as persons. Leaders of groups, pastoral counselors, and fellow parishioners must not demonize the batterer. Rather, as Buber states, the group leader must take on an attitude in which "the 'evil' man is simply one who is commended to him for greater responsibility, one more needy of love."[2] In a world filled with violence, we may need to incarcerate certain individuals. But the primary goal is not to abandon the perpetrator to the often dehumanizing realities of the criminal justice system. It is instead to bring about a re-humanization of even the most brutal criminals. Re-humanization is a central aim of reconciliation.

Although we may view the penitent as one needy of love, we cannot forget the demands of justice. Through the process of ongoing confession, the needs of justice are simultaneously unveiled. As the batterer reveals the nature of the violations, the specific demands of responsibility to his victims become clear. It is the responsibility of the group to help the batterer to list actions to be taken to satisfy justice. It is also the role of the group to ensure that the penitent takes these actions. If a man broke his partner's arm and she was in the hospital for two days, the man should find a means by which he can pay for her hospitalization and her lost wages. The batterer partially satisfies the needs of justice by following the stipulations of his probation, abiding by orders of protection, paying child support on time, and paying the necessary restitution. Satisfaction becomes the concrete manifestation of the ongoing journey of reconciling with the ecclesial and larger community.

As this process continues, the penitent batterer becomes more and more aware of his own capacity to be a responsible person. He comes to understand the mystery of divine love. The love of the community becomes a sign of the love of God. In this way, absolution takes place. Absolution is the moment in which one recognizes that one is loved by God—the mystery of the abundant mercy of the divine is realized. Absolution is the goal of the process of reconciliation. It is the claim of the church that when one realizes that one is fully loved by God, one will also embrace the responsibility to love others.

It has been implied that the healing of the penitent batterer also involves the healing of the survivors of his violence, but it is important to be clear on this point. On the level of individual reconciliation, the needs of the survivor are as important as the needs of the perpetrator. The women and children who have been victimized by men need the full support of the ecclesial community. The community should function as an instrument of protection for women and children. The ecclesial community should establish shelters, provide for assistance in court, and assist in day care. The ecclesial community must also work to create a healing environment in which the survivor may slowly confront the nature of the violation within the context of a supportive community. Although the focus of this study has been primarily on the perpetrator of violence, the healing of the victims is equally important to an adequate reconciliation.[3]

Healing the Interhuman Sphere

Individual healing is necessary for reconciliation, but healing must also occur in the interhuman sphere, the sphere of the "between," that is the space of relating between the violator and the violated, where the violation occurred. In discussing this sphere between humans, the European philosophical tradition has used the word *face* to represent the "other" who calls me to ethical action. Farley uses this term to describe the way in which each person in a relationship may come to encounter the other person in the relationship. In his book *Good and Evil,* Farley describes the difficulty of healing this interhuman sphere: "However much the violator may desire a reparation and even attempt to make things right, the violated face continues its resentful accusation. All efforts to pay the bill fail, disabled in advance by the accusation of the face. The face, thus, exercises a power over both the violator and violated, rending the alienated relation with an unhealable wound."[4] The only possible response is a form of transcending that Farley claims is the tradition's use of the term *forgiveness.* But this term needs to be clearly understood as always facing an "unhealable wound." Farley continues,

> The violated must somehow be released from its resentment and demand on the violator and the violated must somehow be released from its insistence on an impossible reparation. . . . Forgiveness, then, in the sphere of relation is a way of being-together in mutual acceptance which relativizes and places in the background the accusing power of the face. . . . Thus, when the participants in alienated relation experience forgiveness, they are not experiencing simply something from one side or the other of violation but a merger of two transcendings.[5]

What Farley attempts to achieve through the concept of forgiveness is a de-emphasis, but not a forgetting. The violence can never be forgotten, and should never be forgotten, by either member involved in the violation or by the ecclesial community. At the same time, the possibility of the "merger of two transcendings" opens up the possibility of healing the interhuman sphere.

As we have discussed earlier, violence leads to a scarring of the relationship, and this scarring cannot be overlooked. Only through responsibility can one adequately address the scarred relationship. In addition to the scarred relationship, we must also recognize that many people in abusive relationships have grown callous due to extended exposure to violation. Healing the callousness requires tenderness and patience. Through long exposure to tenderness the callousness may begin to fade and the partners may begin to feel again.

Forgiveness may occur when there has been a "merger of two transcendings" that allows for healing. Though forgiveness in the interhuman sphere is possible, accountability and responsibility are untiring voices that always stand in the background of any Christian attempt at forgiveness. Each demands that there is always more to be done. The "face" never disappears; one is always responsible. As Emmanuel Levinas says in *Totality and Infinity*, "The infinity of responsibility denotes not its actual immensity, but a responsibility increasing in the measure that it is assumed; duties become greater in the measure that they are accomplished. The better I accomplish my duty the fewer rights I have; the more I am just the more guilty I am."[6]

This is also true of the frustration that is felt in the process of reconciliation. Once the batterer realizes that he has violated his "lover," he must start on a road that has no final destination, no final place to rest, no place where he will escape from his responsibility. He will find more and more subtle ways in which he participates in the violation of his partner and his children and will recognize his increasingly immense responsibility. It is in this moment that, according to Levinas, the *I* encounters the infinite. As a practical exercise it is sometimes helpful for me, as someone who works with violent men, to sit quietly with the Power and Control Wheel in a meditative way and to ask myself how often I use some of the spokes on the wheel (see chapter 1, Figure 2) with my spouse and my children. I have never been violent with my partner or my children, but I use emotional abuse, I use male privilege, I often blame them for my own failings. This is a very humbling exercise and allows me to recognize Levinas's point for myself, and therefore it enables me to have greater compassion for the violent men with whom I work.

Is Levinas's demand for ultimate responsibility able to be "reconciled" with the Christian symbol of reconciliation? It is certainly not the intent of Levinas, a Jewish French philosopher, to supply a new basis for Christian anthropology or sacramental theology, because any coherent symbol would always break apart under the radical call of responsibility. Ethics, as Levinas understands it, is based on responsibility, and his central image functions in many ways like a new "Protestant principle."[7] This principle of responsibility stands in the background of every relationship. Responsibility refuses any final reconciliation in the form of reunion based on "forgive and forget" and always says "not yet." This does not mean that batterers should never be reunited with their partners, but that any reunion will carry with it ongoing responsibility and the scarring that comes along with deep violation. An appropriate analogy may be that of an alcoholic. Some alcoholics are strong enough and have a supportive enough community that they can go to a party where alcohol is being served and not drink any alcohol. Others cannot be around alcohol, or they will risk falling back into a self-destructive pattern of behavior. A batterer can enter back into a relationship, but he needs the support of a community that believes in him and respects him as a person, and as someone who can be a good partner and a good father, while at the same time he needs a community that holds him accountable and will advocate for the safety of the women and children in his life over the security of his reputation in any situation of further violence.

We have introduced the term *forgiveness* into our discussion of reconciliation. The focus of this book has not been forgiveness, because the role of church leaders and the church community is not to demand that the violated forgive the violator. Instead it is the community's task to create an environment in which both violator and violated may begin the healing process, which may at some point include forgiveness. Though this has not been the focus, it must always be an outcome that would be a desiderata. Yet herein lies one of the most difficult aspects of working in this field: we must not fall into the trap of seeking forgiveness. Setting forgiveness as our goal too easily drags us back into a situation where we lose sight of the cycle of violence and the danger to the battered partner. Reconciliation is the first step, and it must be viewed as enough; for if the woman or the man senses that the real expectation is reunion, we have not learned the lesson Levinas is teaching, and we miss the depth of the problem we have been struggling with throughout this book.

Healing the Community: The Social Level of Reconciliation

In addition to its role as a supportive community for both the perpetrator and the survivor, the ecclesial community must go through its own process of contrition, confession, satisfaction, and absolution. As we have already noted in this project, the church as an institution has been responsible for creating and sustaining many of the deeply influential symbols of our culture. The Christian understandings of violence and marriage have perpetuated violence for many couples during the last two millennia. The ecclesial community should recognize the dangerous dimensions of its historical claims: "marriage is a covenant that cannot be broken," "the man is the head of the home," or "punishment is acceptable within marriage." Contrition involves genuine sorrow over the violations that have occurred. As a representative of God's liberating love on earth, the ecclesial community must be involved in a never-ending self-criticism and a never-ending life of contrition.

The ecclesial community should rethink the religious bond or sacrament of marriage as a means of addressing the complex character of the interhuman sphere. It should embrace the idea of a relationship of mutual respect and cooperation as the center of Christian marriage. It should emphasize the behaviors present in the Equality Wheel. It should stress the mystery of truly encountering the other, and recognize the possibility that violence in a marriage could dissolve this sacred trust. It is through these revisions of its current understanding of Christian marriage that the church will begin to perform its acts of satisfaction as an institution.

Ecclesial responsibility can be seen in a larger context. This larger context is that of societal responsibility. Mike Jackson and

David Garvin have done an excellent job of illustrating this concept in their Coordinated Community Action Model. In this model, they highlight eight social structures that need to be called to greater accountability in reference to domestic violence. Below, I have drawn from their model in gathering a set of suggestions that call these important social systems to greater accountability and acts of satisfaction.

Health Care System
- Develop and utilize safe and effective methods for identification of domestic violence.
- Refrain from overly prescribing sedative drugs to battered women.
- Utilize accountable documentation and reporting protocols for domestic violence.

Justice System
- Regularly disclose relevant statistics on domestic violence case disposition.
- Utilize methods of intervention which do not rely on the victim's involvement.
- Vigorously enforce batterer's compliance and protect women and Children's safety with custody, visitation, and injunctive orders.
- Provide easily accessible and enforceable protection orders.

Education System
- Support and educate teachers to recognize and respond to symptoms of domestic violence in students' lives.
- Teach violence prevention peace-honoring conflict resolution and communication skills.
- Require education about relationships on all levels.

Clergy
- Speak out against domestic violence from the pulpit.
- Routinely assess for domestic violence in premarital and pastoral counseling.

- Seek out and maintain a learning and referral relationship with the domestic. violence coordinated community response system.
- Oppose the use of biblical or theological justification for domestic violence.

Media

- Prioritize subject matter which celebrates peace and nonviolence.
- Educate about the dynamics and consequences of violence, not glorify it.
- Cease labeling domestic violence as "love gone sour," "lover's quarrel," "family spat," etc.

Employers

- Condition batterers continuing employment on remaining nonviolent.
- Intervene against stalkers in the workplace.
- Safeguard battered employee's employment and career by providing flexible schedules, leaves of absence, and establishing enlightened personnel policies.

Government

- Enact laws which define battering as criminal behavior.
- Enact laws which provide courts with progressive consequences in sentencing.
- Heavily tax the sale of weapons and pornography to subsidize sexual and physical violence prevention and intervention efforts.

Social Service Providers

- Design and deliver services which are responsive to battered women and children's needs.
- Require staff to receive training on the etiology and dynamics of domestic violence.
- Shift the focus from "trying to keep the family together at all costs" to safety of battered women and children.[8]

Each sector of society needs to go through a process of contrition, confession, satisfaction, and absolution. What the Coordinated Community Action Model demonstrates is a multi-tiered approach in which each sector of society shows contrition, confession, and acts of satisfaction. Each segment of society must work together if we are to hold violent men accountable, offer these men a sense of hope, and advocate for women and children. Religious organizations should be the leaders in bringing these different segments of society together. Churches can offer a place where business leaders, district attorneys, coaches, educators, political leaders, counselors, and members of the media can meet to discuss how to coordinate these efforts. This should become a part of the church's own process of satisfaction.

Finally, the ecclesial community must offer its model of reconciliation as a supplement to the incarceration system. The practice of reconciliation can work in concert with the criminal justice system as a means of healing violent men. There needs to be an alternative to the dehumanizing role that "justice" plays in our society. By emphasizing compassionate healing that does not dismiss responsibility, the ecclesial community can enter into a dialogue with the larger society about the larger purposes and processes of the justice system. The church can take on its role as a prophetic community by confronting the vengeance implicit in the criminal justice system.

The Dialectic of Reconciliation

We have seen that Thomas Aquinas emphasized four aspects of the sacrament of reconciliation, and it is in the first and last that the dialectical tension of Christian reconciliation is embodied. Aquinas stated that contrition is a lifelong process that calls forth confession and ongoing acts of satisfaction. One's whole life is contrition. Absolution is only properly understood as a moment in which the divine acceptance is made manifest. Absolution is the discovery that God's capacity to love exceeds our capacity to violate one another and to violate our own well-being. God's love exceeds the community's desire for vengeance as well as the penitent's own despair.

God always wills the well-being of each person, regardless of the nature of his or her violation. Within a relational theology and ecclesiology, absolution can become a moment of both healing and responsibility. Reconciliation invites the penitent into the presence of the mystery of God's limitless mercy. At the same time, reconciliation does not support an attitude of "forgive and forget." God does not forget the violation but takes past violations into account in presenting the best opportunities to each of us in the present. As a representative of God in history, the ecclesial community has a responsibility to remember the violations and to encourage and support all those who have been scarred by violence. Reconciliation will remain a classic Christian symbol as long as it discloses permanent possibilities of justice and healing in all three dimensions of human existence. Each of us is called to be a member of this community of healing.

By embracing violent men in their brokenness, the ecclesial community offers witness to the healing power of Christian faith. The women and children who have suffered at the hands of their violent partners or fathers desire a supportive community. The men who are abusive to the people they love also desire a supportive community. Accountability coupled with support addresses the tragic flaw of violent men. It is essential that communities of faith advocate for and support women and children who have suffered abuse. But this advocacy is not enough; the community must also call men to conversion. Only through working with the men who are violent does the community strike at the root of the violence. It is only through accountability on all three levels of relationship (individual, interhuman, and social) that a transformation to a nonviolent society is possible. What greater gift could one give to the world than to participate in the transformation of hatred, insecurity, and abusive power into love, respect, and safety? Remember Martin Buber's admonition: the "evil" man is simply one in greater need of love. Peace comes to the world one person at a time. Each angry, violent soul who finds the path to nonviolence leaves in his wake a world no longer afraid. We can help to eliminate fear in our homes if we will walk the difficult journey of self-discovery with the most violent men in our communities. On this journey we will also discover the wisdom of the divine mystery.

Appendix 1
Indicators That a Man May Kill His Partner

1. Threats of Homicide or Suicide.

The batterer who has threatened to kill himself, his partner, the children, or his partner's relatives must be considered extremely dangerous.

2. Fantasies of Homicide or Suicide.

The more the batterer has developed a fantasy about how, when, or where to kill, the more dangerous he may be. The batterer who has previously acted out part of a homicide or suicide fantasy may be invested in killing as a viable "solution" to his problems. As in suicide assessment, the more detailed the plan and the more available the method, the greater the risk.

3. Weapons.

Where a batterer possesses weapons and has used them or has threatened to use them in the past in his assaults on the battered women, the children, or himself, his access to those weapons increases his potential for lethal assault. The use of guns is a strong predictor of homicide. If a batterer has a history of arson or the threat of arson, fire should be considered a weapon.

4. "Ownership" of the battered partner.

The batterer who says "Death before divorce!" or "You belong to me and will never belong to another!" may be stating his fundamental belief that the woman has no right to life separate from him. A batterer who believes he is absolutely entitled to his female partner, her services, her obedience and her loyalty, no matter what, is likely to be life endangering.

5. Centrality of the partner.

A man who idolizes his female partner, or depends heavily on her to organize and sustain his life, or who has isolated himself from all other community, may retaliate against a partner who decides to end the relationship. He rationalizes that her "betrayal" justifies his lethal retaliation.

6. Separation violence.

When a batterer believes that he is about to lose his partner, if he cannot envision life without her or if the separation causes him great despair or rage, he may choose to kill.

7. Escalation of batterer risk.

A less obvious indicator of increasing danger may be the sharp escalation of personal risk taken by the batterer; when a batterer begins to act without regard to the legal or social consequences that previously constrained his violence, chances of lethal assault increase significantly.

8. Hostage-taking.

A hostage-taker is at high risk of inflicting homicide. Between 75 percent and 90 percent of all hostage takings in the United States are related to domestic violence situations.

9. Depression.

Where a batterer has been acutely depressed and sees little hope for moving beyond the depression, he may be a candidate for homicide and suicide. Research shows that many men who are hospitalized for depression have homicidal fantasies directed at family members.

10. Repeated outreach to law enforcement.

Partner or spousal homicide almost always occurs in a context of historical violence. Prior calls to the police indicate elevated risk of life-threatening conduct.

11. Access to the battered woman or to family members.

If the batterer cannot find her, he cannot kill her. If he does not have access to the children, he cannot use them as a means of access to the battered woman. Careful safety planning and police assistance are required for those times when contact is required, for example, court appearances and custody exchanges.

Adapted from Barbara Hart, "Assessing Whether Batterers Will Kill," Pennsylvania Coalition Against Domestic Violence, 1990.

Appendix 2
Accountability

A man who has battered a woman becomes accountable when:

1. he has acknowledged to the battered woman and to their community of friends that he has assaulted and controlled a woman, and that he has committed acts of violence against her;
2. he has admitted the pattern of abusive control that tyrannized her;
3. he recognizes that his behavior was unprovoked and inexcusable;
4. he knows his behavior was criminal;
5. he understands his behavior was not caused by stress, chemical dependency, or any other outside factor;
6. he knows he was not out of control;
7. he admits that he intended to control or punish her;
8. he deeply regrets his actions and is horrified;
9. he recognizes the pain and suffering he visited upon her;
10. he accepts full responsibility for his acts;
11. he acknowledges this without expectations of approval from her;
12. he understands he is not entitled to her forgiveness;
13. he recognizes that the woman may never trust him again and may remain afraid of him forever;
14. he can enumerate the losses suffered by her and her family;
15. he does not expect protection for his name;
16. he realizes he needs the help of his family, his friends, and his community to prevent further use of violence;
17. he knows that he needs to find others to support him in nonviolence;

18. he knows clearly that there is nothing in the relationship of the woman that caused his battery;
19. he knows he is at risk of battering any woman in the future;
20. he realizes that the battered woman should not have to hear any of the above points from him, unless she desires to hear it;
21. he agrees to limit contact with her, her friends, and her family;
22. he agrees to stop chasing and tracking her;
23. he agrees to avoid the places she frequents and to provide her with plenty of space away from him;
24. he agrees to stop collecting information about her;
25. he understands he needs to pay restitution, which could mean child support or alimony if she desires, and he agrees to support her in this restitution as long as she needs it, to replace the losses she has sustained;
26. and finally, he refuses to manipulate their children to discredit her.

Adapted from Barbara Hart, Pennsylvania Coalition Against Domestic Violence.

Appendix 3
Control Log: Men's Education Groups

Name _____

Date _____

1. Actions: Briefly describe the situation and the actions you used to control your partner (statements, gestures, tone of voice, physical contact, facial expressions).

_____

_____

_____

_____

_____

2. Intents and Beliefs: What did you want to happen in this situation? What belief do you have that supports your actions and intents?

_____

_____

_____

3. Feelings: What feelings were you having?

_____

_____

_____

4. Minimization, Denial, and Blame: In what ways did you minimize or deny your actions or blame her?

_____

_____

_____

_____

_____

5. Effects: What was the impact of your action?

On you _____

On her _____

On others _____

6. Past Violence: How did your past use of violence affect this situation?

_____

_____

_____

_____

_____

7. Noncontrolling Behaviors: What could you have done differently?

_____

_____

_____

_____

_____

Appendix 4
An Annotated Website Bibliography

Websites with General Information about Domestic Violence

Family Violence Prevention Fund

http://endabuse.org

This is a website run by an international organization attempting to educate people about family violence. The site offers current news on domestic violence both in the United States and overseas.

National Clearinghouse on Marital and Date Rape

http://members.aol.com/ncmdr/index.html

An excerpt from the site: "Our mission is to bring about social, legal, political, psychological, economic, and religious change through our vast resource network of information and support, in order to make intimate relationships truly egalitarian."

National Coalition for Domestic Abuse Awareness

http://www.domesticabuseawareness.org

This site contains links to information on domestic abuse in each state.

Websites on Treatment of Batterers

Abuse-Free Family of Mail Lists

http://blainn.cc/abuse-free

This website offers abusers an online support community. An excerpt from the list explaining the nature of the listserv:

Participation in Abuse-free is restricted to recovering spouse abusers—that is, individuals who have exhibited controlling, intimidating, or violent behaviors in intimate relationships, and are making a sincere effort to change and to build an abuse-free life—and those who are uncertain but concerned that they might be abusive. Therapists, law enforcement officials, abuse survivors, clergy, celebrities, members of the media, elected or appointed government officials, advocates, activists, and all others are welcome to participate on the list if they meet these qualifications and are willing to abide by the rules of the list. If not, they are welcome to consider participation in an affiliated list they might qualify for.

Batterer Intervention Programs
http://www.vaw.umn.edu/bip.asp
This website contains documents evaluating batterers' treatment programs.

National Criminal Justice Reference Service
http://www.ncjrs.org
This website includes excellent resources on batterers' treatment programs, especially the government document *Batterer Intervention: Program Approaches and Criminal Justice Strategies*, by Kerry Healy, Christine Smith, and Chris O'Sullivan. Access these websites through the "victims of crime" link and then follow the "domestic violence" link (both are in the left-hand sidebar).

Websites on Community Responses to Domestic Violence

Campaign for Forgiveness Research
http://www.forgiving.org
This website offers information about current research in the area of forgiveness.

Domestic Violence Hotlines and Resources
http://www.feminist.org/911/crisis.html
This website includes hotlines and crisis resources for almost every part of the country.

Notes

Preface

1. For three years I worked for a batterers' treatment agency, the Project to End Abuse through Counseling and Education (P.E.A.C.E.) in Nashville, Tennessee. The stories that are woven throughout this project are combinations of individual stories I heard from hundreds of different men who were court-ordered into this program during the years 1992 through 1994. The program uses the Duluth curriculum based on the Power and Control Wheel. This curriculum was expanded into a year-long curriculum, which I co-authored with Donna Bridges and Mark Justad in 1995.

Chapter 1

1. David Tracy, *The Analogical Imagination: Christian Theology and the Culture of Pluralism* (New York: Crossroad, 1981), 108.

2. We return to the root of reconciliation below. Also note the discussion of reconciliation in Pamela Cooper-White's book, *The Cry of Tamar: Violence against Women and the Church's Response* (Minneapolis: Fortress Press, 1995), 261–62.

3. David Tracy, *Plurality and Ambiguity: Hermeneutics, Religion, Hope* (Chicago: University of Chicago Press, 1994), 17–19.

4. The term *ecclesial community* will be used throughout the text to refer to the community of people committed to the prophetic gospel tradition of Christianity. This tradition attempts to live out the virtues of compassion, justice, and love professed by Jesus of Nazareth. This community is a part of the larger Christian church but does not refer exclusively to the hierarchical institutional church per se.

5. Edward Farley's understanding of deep symbols, which parallels Tracy's concept of the classic, is discussed at the beginning of chapter 4. See also Edward Farley, *Deep Symbols: Their Postmodern Effacement and Reclamation* (Valley Forge, Pa.: Trinity Press International, 1996).

6. Helen Prejean, C.S.J., *Dead Man Walking: An Eyewitness Account of the Death Penalty in the United States* (New York: Vintage, 1993). Some of the ideas discussed appear only in the film adaptation of the book and not in the book itself.

7. Tracy, *Plurality and Ambiguity*, 69.

8. This story combines several real stories that I heard in my years as a counselor of men convicted of battering. I saw these men weekly in group therapy and also in court when I worked as the Court Advocate for the Project to End Abuse through Counseling and Education (P.E.A.C.E.). The names used are not the names of the men in the program.

9. Patricia Tjaden and Nancy Thoennes, "Prevalence, Incidence, and Consequences of Violence against Women: Findings from the National Violence against Women Survey" (Washington, D.C.: U.S. Department of Justice, 1998), 2. The summary report of the National Violence against Women Survey can be found at http://www.ncjrs.org/txtfiles/172837.txt.

10. The use of the term *erotic* as the adjectival modifier of the relationship is to emphasize that these relationships are not limited by the social conventions of marriage, cohabitation, or sexual intimacy. I use the term *erotic* to connote an intense erotic love, whether felt or acted on by either person in the relationship. Most intimate violence occurs within the context of a dating, marital, or co-habitational arrangement in which some form of sexual intimacy is involved. All of these components emerge as important aspects of the relationship and its dynamics, as we will discuss below.

11. Christie Cozad Neuger and James Newton Poling, eds., *The Care of Men* (Nashville: Abingdon, 1997), 140.

12. Lenore E. Walker, *The Battered Woman Syndrome* (New York: Springer, 1984).

13. Lenore E. Walker, *The Battered Woman* (New York: Harper and Row, 1979), 55–70.

14. Though Walker's theory, supported by attachment theory, explains some of the cases of intimate violence, not all relationships function on a cyclical model. Rather, the violence in these relationships continues in an intermittent way. Dutton claims that Walker's theory needs to be supplemented with a theory of intermittent reinforcement and traumatic bonding. He states, "The present data suggests that intermittency of abuse, not a battering cycle per se, is a major determinant of the battered woman syndrome. Whereas a cycle of violence perspective describes violence as going through predictable (and mood-driven)

cycles, the term intermittency, as defined in this research, simply indicates that extreme positive and negative behaviors occur with temporal contiguity; they need to be neither cyclical nor predictable." Donald C. Dutton, *The Domestic Assault of Women: Psychological and Criminal Justice Perspectives* (Vancouver: University of British Columbia Press, 1995), 212–13.

15. See Walker, *The Battered Woman* and *The Battered Woman Syndrome*. This psychological complex, which has been used in the defense of women in courtrooms in recent years, creates a situation in which women remain with their abusive partners not because of masochistic personality disorders as was proposed by some psychologists in the early 1980s, but because they have developed a psychological coping mechanism to a situation that has no good alternatives.

16. John Bowlby, *Attachment and Loss*, vol. 2: *Separation* (New York: Basic, 1973), 235, cited in Dutton, *Domestic Assault*, 149. Emphasis by Dutton.

17. Dutton, *Domestic Assault*, 159–60.

18. Ibid., 190.

19. Ibid., 42.

20. An excellent resource on child abuse is Mary Edna Helfer, Ruth S. Kemper, and Richard D. Krugman, eds., *The Battered Child* (5th ed.; Chicago: University of Chicago Press, 1997). It is important to note that child abuse happens not only at the hands of fathers but also at the hands of mothers. One of the most riveting stories of child abuse at the hands of a mother is David Pelzer's *A Child Called It* (Deerfield Beach, Fla.: Health Communications, 1995).

21. Tjaden and Thoennes, "Prevalence, Incidence, and Consequences of Violence against Women," 4.

22. Women are also more likely to be killed by their ex-partner while seeking help from the legal system or while leaving. See Joan C. Parker, Barbara Hart, and Jane Stueling, *Seeking Justice: Legal Advocacy Principles and Practice* (Harrisburg: Pennsylvania Coalition Against Domestic Violence, 1992).

23. Ann Jones, *Next Time, She'll Be Dead: Battering and How to Stop It* (Boston: Beacon, 1994), 72.

Chapter 2

1. "Sentence in Maryland Wife Murder Stirs Row," *Facts on File World News Digest*, November 17, 1994, 859-D3, cited in

Judith A. Boss, *Analyzing Moral Issues* (Mountain View, Calif.: Mayfield, 1999), 692.

2. Among the many texts that have challenged the foundational assumptions of patriarchal culture and theology are the following: Mary Daly, *Pure Lust: Elemental Feminist Philosophy* (New York: Harper Collins, 1984); Joanne Carlson Brown and Carole R. Bohn, eds., *Christianity, Patriarchy, and Abuse: A Feminist Critique* (New York: Pilgrim, 1989); and Rosemary Radford Ruether, *Sexism and God-Talk: Toward a Feminist Theology* (Boston: Beacon, 1983). These texts share a criticism of the assumptions that masculinity, understood as a capacity to control and dominate others, permeates the philosophical and theological texts of previous generations of thinkers and that hierarchical, controlling, individualistic tendencies of patriarchy should be replaced by a more egalitarian, relational mutuality as a basis for everything from epistemology to Christology and ecclesiology.

3. Demie Kurz, "Physical Assaults by Spouses a Major Social Problem," in Richard J. Gelles and Donileen R. Loseke, eds., *Current Controversies on Family Violence* (Newbury Park, Calif.: Sage, 1993), 90.

4. Ibid.

5. For some important trends in the field of interpreting the law surrounding domestic violence, see N. Zoe Hilton, ed., *Legal Responses to Wife Assault: Current Trends and Evaluation* (Newberry Park, Calif.: Sage, 1993).

6. The FBI Uniform Crime Report can be most easily accessed at www.fbi.gov/ucr/00cius.htm.

7. Freud uses gender-specific language when he addresses human violence. It is not clear whether Freud specifically intended to use male pronouns or gender-neutral pronouns. When reading quotations from Freud included in this chapter, the use of *him, his,* or *he* seems appropriate to the gendered character of violence that we wish to address. For the reasons above, I have maintained Freud's use of male pronouns, as they appear to be accurate in indicating both Freud's perspective and the phenomenon as it is most likely to be experienced in history. See Sigmund Freud, *Civilization and Its Discontents,* trans. Joan Riviere (1929), in *Great Books of the Western World,* ed. Robert M. Hutchins (Chicago: Encyclopedia Britannica, 1952), 782–83.

8. Ibid., 787. Italics mine. I wish to emphasize that Freud was well aware that many thinkers found his identification of an instinct toward aggression and death to be untenable because of their desire to maintain the human as fundamentally good. I do not wish to present a naïve

notion of human goodness, as this is untenable in reference to the ongoing destruction that humans continue to inflict on other humans and on the rest of creation. At the same time, the Freudian analysis does not allow for the possibility that some people are not tied to violence as necessary behavior.

9. Myriam Miedzian, *Boys Will Be Boys: Breaking the Link between Masculinity and Violence* (New York: Doubleday, 1991), 49. One must also note the phallic connection present within the hydraulic model. It restates an idea that many men use to justify their sense of entitlement. Many men claim there is a hydraulic pressure that lies behind their "need" for sex. The phallocentric culture certainly views many actions that men take as being related to this hydraulic model besides their need to be violent, and in all these cases the sense of responsibility is lessened or denied because of the building pressure.

10. Donald G. Dutton, *The Domestic Assault of Women: Psychological and Criminal Justice Perspectives* (Vancouver: University of British Columbia Press, 1995), 79.

11. René Girard, *Violence and the Sacred*, trans. Patrick Gregory (Baltimore: Johns Hopkins University Press, 1977). Only one aspect of Girard's argument will be examined. Certain fundamental issues such as mimetic desire and Girard's specific use of Freud will be omitted in order to focus on the issue of vengeance as the central element in Girard's understanding.

12. This distinction between reciprocal violence and sacred violence is a theme that carries through many of the ideas of the theorists cited in this chapter. We will see this in Sherman Stanage's phenomenological description as well as in James Gilligan's proposals, found at the end of this chapter.

13. It is important to note here that we will be attempting to show that it is not "sacred violence" toward a specific member of the community that will reconcile the community to itself. Rather, compassion, responsibility, and hope will help to reconcile the violent offender to the rest of the community and so help to reconcile the community to itself.

14. Girard, *Violence and the Sacred*, 13. It is important to note that there is some truth to Girard's insight that some people "cannot suppress" their desire to commit an act of violence on those near to them. This is why we propose that men be separated from their families for a time after incidents of intimate violence, not immediately reunited.

15. Ibid., 15.

16. Suchocki makes a similar, though not identical, claim in her recent book *The Fall to Violence*. Suchocki's primary concern is with the doctrine of "original sin". She uses many of the same materials, combining them with a foundation in process thought which allows her to retrieve the symbol of original sin as an inherent potential for violence. Marjorie Hewitt Suchocki, *The Fall to Violence: Original Sin in Relational Theology* (New York: Continuum, 1995).

17. E. O. Wilson, *On Human Nature* (New York: Bantam, 1982), 108, cited in Miedzian, *Boys Will Be Boys*, 49–50.

18. In contrast, our society appears to make the trigger mechanism more sensitive through subcultures that condone violence. Children begin to thrive on quick reactions of violence based in revenge or the elimination of evil. This is explored in greater detail by James Gilligan in his notion that society creates a culture of violence that it uses to maintain certain political and economic imbalances. See note 30, below, and James Gilligan, *Violence: Reflections on a National Epidemic* (New York: Vintage, 1997), 187–89. This can also be seen in James William Gibson's book *Warrior Dreams: Violence and Manhood in Post-Vietnam America* (New York: Hill and Wang, 1994). Gibson discusses the subculture of violence present in the lives of Vietnam veterans. He exposes the glamorization of violence in film, literature, and magazines. According to this subculture, being a man requires one to be violent. If this is the case, it requires us to be aware of men who have been influenced by these violence-driven subcultures. The glamorization of violence is another factor that the church should be cognizant of when formulating its understanding of reconciliation.

19. Miedzian, *Boys Will Be Boys*, 74.

20. Ibid., 74–76.

21. Stephen Boyd, *The Men We Long to Be: Beyond Domination to a New Christian Understanding of Manhood* (New York: Harper Collins, 1995), 52.

22. National Institute of Mental Health, 1982 Annual report, "Television and Behavior: Ten Years of Scientific Progress and Implications for the Eighties," 6, cited in Miedzian, *Boys Will Be Boys*, 216.

23. Brandon S. Centerwall, "Television and the Development of the Superego: Pathways to Violence," in Colette Chiland and Gerald Young, eds., *Children and Violence* (Northvale, N.J.: Aronson, 1994), 185–87.

24. This can be seen in the chart in Stephen Boyd, *The Men We Long to Be*, 52. See also Mary Pipher, *Reviving Ophelia: Saving the Selves of Adolescent Girls* (New York: Ballentine, 1994).

25. There are several good books on the issue of dating violence, including Maureen A. Pirog-Good and Jan E. Stets, eds., *Violence in Dating Relationships* (Westport, Conn.: Praeger, 1989), and Barrie Levy, ed., *Dating Violence: Young Women in Danger* (Seattle: Seal, 1998).

26. Sherman M. Stanage, "Violatives: Modes and Themes of Violence," in *Reason and Violence: Philosophical Investigations* (Totowa, N.J.: Littlefield, Adams, 1974), 213.

27. Ibid., 216.

28. The socially constructed view of women who kill their partners in "self-defense" is still unsettled. A debate exists as to whether it is constructive violence (self-defense) or destructive violence (premeditated murder). On this subject, see Lenore E. Walker, *The Battered Woman* (New York: Harper and Row, 1979), 220–21; and N. Zoe Hilton, ed., *Legal Responses to Wife Assault: Current Trends and Evaluation* (Newbury Park, Calif.: Sage, 1993), chs. 9 and 10.

29. U.S. Department of Justice, Bureau of Justice Statistics Bulletin, 1997 annual report (NCJ 167247).

30. Gilligan, *Violence*. It is necessary to point out that Gilligan's position on shame differs in significant ways from the definitions of shame in much of the men's movement literature. See Robert Bly, *Iron John: A Book about Men* (Reading, Mass.: Addison Wesley, 1990), and Sam Keen, *Fire in the Belly: On Being a Man* (New York: Bantam, 1991).

31. Gilligan, *Violence*, 12. This claim may appear to many observers to excuse violent behavior, justifying the crimes of men against women, children, and each other. I, with Gilligan, wish to stress that this proposal is in no way meant to exonerate or justify the behavior of violent men; it is rather a means of understanding this behavior, toward the goal of prevention. As Gilligan says, "It is easier and less threatening to condemn violence (morally and legally) so as to punish it, rather than seeking its cause and working to prevent it" (ibid., 24).

32. Interestingly, Girard's theory of "criminal violence" and "sacred violence" and Gilligan's proposal converge. Girard claims that "criminal violence further perpetuates violence because it creates a desire for revenge." Gilligan understands the punishment meted out by our penal system as having the same effect as Girard's "criminal violence."

33. Gilligan, *Violence*, 184.

34. Ibid., 185–86.

35. The list is as follows: (1) punishing more and more people; (2) outlawing drugs that inhibit violence, while legalizing drugs that may stimulate violence; (3) manipulating the tax laws to increase economic

disparity; (4) depriving the poor of access to education; (5) perpetuating the caste divisions in society; (6) exposing the public to entertainment that glorifies violence; (7) making lethal weapons easily available; (8) maximizing the asymmetry of the social roles of men and women; (9) encouraging prejudice against homosexuality; (10) legitimizing the exposure of children to violence in the form of corporal punishment; and (11) regulating the economy to ensure that unemployment will never be abolished. For a further discussion of each of these points, see ibid., 187–89.

Chapter 3

1. It is clear that the initial social function of marriage was procreation and preservation of the social order. Though this has become less important since the seventeenth century, marriage's influence on our society remains powerful. Marriage continues to function as an institution of social regulation.

2. Wife beating as a metaphor for God's punishment of Israel was used by Hosea and influenced by the later prophets. This argument is clearly outlined in Renita J. Weems, *Battered Love: Marriage, Sex, and Violence in the Hebrew Prophets* (Minneapolis: Fortress Press, 1995), 45–53.

3. Ibid., 51; emphasis mine.

4. Rosemary Radford Ruether, *Christianity and the Making of the Modern Family* (Boston: Beacon, 2000), 5–6.

5. Ibid., 7.

6. Steven Ozment, *When Fathers Ruled: Family Life in Reformation Europe* (Cambridge: Harvard University Press, 1983), 77, quoted in Mary Potter Engel, "Historical Theology and Violence against Women," in Carol J. Adams and Marie M. Fortune, eds., *Violence against Women and Children: A Christian Theological Sourcebook* (New York: Continuum, 1995), 255.

7. For a more generous appraisal of the Catholic perspective on marriage, see Evelyn E. Whitehead and James D. Whitehead, *Marrying Well: Stages on the Journey of Christian Marriage* (New York: Doubleday, 1983).

8. John M. Johnson and Denise M. Bondurant, "Revisiting the 1982 Church Response Survey," in Adams and Fortune, eds., *Violence against Women and Children*, 425.

9. Although many different rites are used in contemporary wedding ceremonies, involving Christ in the heart of the marriage relationships

places the latter at the very center of Christianity's whole cultural meaning, even in less sacramental Christian traditions. See, for example, Robert W. Jenson, "The Sacraments," *Christian Dogmatics*, vol. 2, ed. Carl E. Braaten and Robert W. Jenson (Philadelphia: Fortress Press, 1984), 383–85. The marriage rite is quoted from Joseph Martos, *Doors to the Sacred: A Historical Introduction to Sacraments in the Catholic Church* (Garden City, N.Y., Doubleday, 1982), 396.

10. Mark Knox, "Fellowship Declines to Debate SBC," *Baptist Standard* (July 8, 1998); see also "Southern Baptists Declare Wife Should 'Submit' to Her Husband," *New York Times* (June 10, 1998).

11. Diana E. H. Russell, *Rape in Marriage* (Bloomington: Indiana University Press, 1982), 17–19.

12. Ibid., 375–82.

13. This story, related in Russell's book *Rape in Marriage*, 295–96, was first reported in "Marine to Be Tried for Wife's Rape," *Tri-Valley Herald* (Livermore, Calif.), April 11, 1980.

14. Many criticisms of this are present in contemporary theology, especially in the reconstructions of theodicy. See especially Wendy Farley, *Tragic Vision and Divine Compassion: A Contemporary Theodicy* (Louisville, Ky.: Westminster John Knox, 1990), ch. 1, and Kathleen M. Sands, *Escape from Paradise: Evil and Tragedy in Feminist Theology* (Minneapolis: Fortress Press, 1994).

15. Farley, *Tragic Vision and Divine Compassion*, 21.

16. An excellent recent study of the way in which the images of God have been challenged by feminist theology and the potential for new images is found in Laurel C. Schneider's book, *Re-Imagining the Divine: Confronting the Backlash against Feminist Theology* (Cleveland: Pilgrim, 1999).

17. Mary Daly, *Outercourse: The Bedazzling Voyage* (New York: Harper Collins, 1992), 152.

Chapter 4

1. Edward Farley, *Deep Symbols: Their Postmodern Effacement and Reclamation* (Valley Forge, Pa.: Trinity Press International, 1996).

2. Ibid., 26.

3. Ibid., 4.

4. One can see this theme played out most clearly in the twelfth-century atonement theory of Anselm of Canterbury in his *Cur Deus Homo*. In this feudal reading of atonement, someone must be punished

for the offense against the divine. This monarchical notion of reconciliation as a punishment that satisfies divine justice lingers in our theological tradition to this day.

5. Wendy Farley and Kathleen Sands offer insight on the issue of how the tradition has addressed violence and its problematic character. See Wendy Farley, *Tragic Vision and Divine Compassion: A Contemporary Theodicy* (Louisville, Ky.: Westminster John Knox, 1990), and Kathleen M. Sands, *Escape from Paradise: Evil and Tragedy in Feminist Theology* (Minneapolis: Fortress Press, 1994)

6. See the consideration of the Holocaust of Germany in Hannah Arendt's *Eichmann in Jerusalem: A Report on the Banality of Evil* (New York: Viking Penguin, 1963). Also see a consideration of the use of rape as a form of ethnic cleansing in Alexandra Stiglmayer, ed., *Mass Rape: The War against Women in Bosnia-Herzegovina,* trans. Marion Faber (Lincoln: University of Nebraska Press, 1994).

7. In the absence of this vision, theologians like Wendy Farley, Kathleen Sands, Peter Hodgson, Gordon Kaufman, David Tracy, and Edward Farley, to name only a sampling, have begun to reconstruct a vision of God and of evil that moves away from traditional theodicies and toward a new vision of the relationship between humanity and God. See Farley, *Tragic Vision and Divine Compassion;* Sands, *Escape from Paradise*; Gordon D. Kaufman, *In Face of Mystery: A Constructive Theology* (Cambridge: Harvard University Press, 1993); Peter C. Hodgson, *God in History: Shapes of Freedom* (Nashville: Abingdon, 1989); David Tracy, *Plurality and Ambiguity: Hermeneutics, Religion, Hope* (Chicago: University of Chicago Press, 1994); and Edward Farley, *Good and Evil: Interpreting a Human Condition* (Minneapolis: Fortress Press, 1990), and *Divine Empathy: A Theology of God* (Minneapolis: Fortress Press, 1996).

8. Note the connection to the 1982 church survey of pastors cited in the previous chapter.

9. Note the discussion in Jones's text *Embodying Forgiveness*, especially ch. 4. Gregory Jones, *Embodying Forgiveness: A Theological Analysis* (Grand Rapids, Mich.: Eerdmans, 1995).

10. Ladislas Orsy, *The Evolving Church and the Sacrament of Penance* (Denville, N.J.: Dimension, 1978), 32.

11. Hugh Connelly, *The Irish Penitentials and Their Significance for the Sacrament of Penance Today* (Portland: Four Courts, 1995), 14–15.

12. Thomas Aquinas, *The Summa Theologica of St. Thomas Aquinas*, trans. the Fathers of the English Dominican Province (2nd rev. ed.; Allen, Tex.: Thomas More, 1981), vol. 5, q. 84–89.

13. H. Denzinger and A. Schoenmetzer, *Enchridion Symbolorum: Definitionum De Rubis Fidei et Morum* (Freiburg: Herder, 1976), 897.

14. Peter Lombard and Bonaventure disagreed with many other theologians during this period, claiming that only perfect contrition could satisfy the requirements for penance. Aquinas, *The Summa Theologica,* vol. 5, Supplement, q.1, art. 3. There are some similarities between the distinctions drawn by Aquinas between *attritio* and *contritio* and those of Lawrence Kohlberg in his theory of moral development. Fear of punishment appears in Kohlberg's early stages, and only in his later stages do humans act morally based on a more universal or individual sense of the right or the good. See Lawrence Kohlberg, *The Psychology of Moral Development: The Nature and Validity of Moral Stages* (San Francisco: Harper and Row, 1984).

15. James Gilligan, *Violence: Reflections on a National Epidemic* (New York: Random House, 1997), 50–52.

16. Ibid., 51.

17. See p. 15.

18. Lenore E. Walker, *The Battered Woman* (New York: Harper and Row, 1979), 93.

19. Aquinas, *The Summa Theologica*, Supplement, vol. 5, q.4. art. 1. My emphasis.

20. Thomas Aquinas, *Summa Contra Gentiles, An Annotated Translation,* trans. Joseph Rickaby, S.J. (Westminster, Md.: Carroll, 1950), bk. 4, q.72, 394.

21. Aquinas does allow for the possibility of perfect absolution, by which he means that one so hates the violation that one will not suffer eternal damnation nor is one required to do any further act of satisfaction. This is possible but is not the normal situation, according to him. Thomas Aquinas, *Summa Contra Gentiles*, bk. 4, q.72, 395.

22. Recidivism rates among violent offenders average approximately 40 percent, according to the U.S. Department of Justice. See *Bureau of Justice Statistics Special Report: Recidivism of Prisoners Released in 1983,* doc. NCJ-116261 (Washington, D.C.: U.S. Department of Justice, 1989), 5.

Chapter 5

1. An excellent new book offers step-by-step instructions on how to establish and run a batterers' treatment program. See David J. Decker, *Stopping the Violence: A Group Model to Change Men's Abusive Attitudes*

and Behaviors (New York: Haworth Maltreatment and Trauma, 1999). This book is a resource that every pastor should have in her or his library. The model for a batterers' group should be one of accountability and support.

2. Martin Buber, *I and Thou,* trans. Ronald Gregor Smith (New York: Scribner's Sons, 1958), 109.

3. For analysis of the church's responsibility to battered and abused women and children, see the following: Pamela Cooper-White, *The Cry of Tamar: Violence against Women and the Church's Response* (Minneapolis: Fortress Press, 1995); Carol J. Adams and Marie M. Fortune, eds., *Violence against Women and Children: A Christian Theological Sourcebook* (New York: Continuum, 1995); Carol J. Adams, *Woman Battering* (Minneapolis: Fortress Press, 1994); Joanne Carlson Brown and Carole R. Bohn, eds., *Christianity, Patriarchy, and Abuse: A Feminist Critique* (New York: Pilgrim, 1989); Elisabeth Schüssler Fiorenza and Mary Shawn Copeland eds., *Violence against Women* (Concilium, vol. 1; Maryknoll, N.Y.: Orbis, 1994).

4. Edward Farley, *Good and Evil: Interpreting a Human Condition* (Minneapolis: Fortress Press, 1990), 248.

5. Ibid., 248.

6. Emmanuel Levinas, *Totality and Infinity: An Essay in Exteriority,* trans. Alphonso Lingis (Pittsburgh: Duquesne University Press, 1969), 244.

7. Paul Tillich, *The Dynamics of Faith* (New York: Harper and Row, 1957), 29.

8. Mike Jackson and David Garvin, Domestic Violence Institute of Michigan. You can order copies of the Coordinated Community Action Model and other helpful resources from Alternatives to Domestic Aggression, Catholic Social Services of Washtenaw County, 4925 Packard Road, Ann Arbor, MI 48108-1521; tel. (734) 971-9781; website: http://comnet.org/adacss; email: adainfo@csswashtenaw.org.

Selected Bibliography

Adams, Carol J. *Woman Battering*. Creative Pastoral Care and Counseling. Minneapolis: Fortress Press, 1994.

Adams, Carol J., and Marie M. Fortune, eds. *Violence against Women and Children: A Christian Theological Sourcebook*. New York: Continuum, 1995.

Aquinas, Thomas. *Summa Contra Gentiles, An Annotated Translation*. Translated by Joseph Rickaby, S.J. Westminster, Md: Carroll, 1950.

———. *The Summa Theologica of St. Thomas Aquinas*. 2nd and revised edition. Translated by the Fathers of the English Dominican Province. Allen, Tex.: Thomas More, 1981.

Augustine. *The Confessions*. Translated by Maria Boulding, O.S.B. New York: Random House, 1997.

Bailie, Gil. *Violence Unveiled: Humanity at the Crossroads*. New York: Crossroad, 1995.

Boyd, Stephen. *The Men We Long to Be: Beyond Domination to a New Christian Understanding of Manhood*. New York: Harper Collins, 1995.

Brown, Joanne Carlson, and Carole R. Bohn, eds. *Christianity, Patriarchy, and Abuse: A Feminist Critique*. New York: Pilgrim, 1989.

Brownmiller, Susan. *Against Our Will: Men, Women, and Rape*. New York: Simon and Schuster, 1975.

Bussert, Joy K. *Battered Women: From a Theology of Suffering to an Ethic of Empowerment*. New York: Lutheran Church of America, 1986.

Butler, Judith. *Bodies that Matter: On the Discursive Limits of "Sex."* New York: Routledge, 1993.

Connolly, Hugh. *The Irish Penitentials and Their Significance for the Sacrament of Penance Today*. Portland, Ore.: Four Courts, 1995.

Cooper-White, Pamela. *The Cry of Tamar: Violence against Women and the Church's Response.* Minneapolis: Fortress Press, 1995.

Counts, Dorothy Ayer, et al. *Sanctions and Sanctuary: Cultural Perspectives on the Beating of Wives.* Oxford: Westview, 1992.

Dallen, James. *The Reconciling Community: The Rite of Penance.* New York: Pueblo, 1986.

Daly, Mary. *Gyn/Ecology: A Metaethics of Radical Feminism.* Boston: Beacon, 1978.

———. *Pure Lust: Elemental Feminist Philosophy.* New York: Harper Collins, 1984.

———. *Outercourse: The Bedazzling Voyage.* New York: Harper Collins, 1992.

Decker, David J. *Stopping the Violence: A Group Model to Change Men's Abusive Attitudes and Behaviors.* New York: Haworth Maltreatment and Trauma, 1999.

Doggett, Maeve E. *Marriage, Wife-Beating and the Law in Victorian England.* Columbia: University of South Carolina Press, 1993.

Dutton, Donald G. *The Domestic Assault of Women: Psychological and Criminal Justice Perspectives.* Vancouver: University of British Columbia Press, 1995.

Farley, Edward. *Good and Evil: Interpreting a Human Condition.* Minneapolis: Fortress Press, 1990.

———. *Deep Symbols: Their Postmodern Effacement and Reclamation.* Valley Forge, Pa.: Trinity Press International, 1996.

———. *Divine Empathy: A Theology of God.* Minneapolis: Fortress Press, 1996.

Farley, Wendy. *Tragic Vision and Divine Compassion: A Contemporary Theodicy.* Louisville, Ky.: Westminster John Knox, 1990.

Foucault, Michel. *Discipline and Punish: The Birth of the Prison.* Translated by Alan Sheridan. New York: Vintage, 1979.

Freud, Sigmund. *Civilization and Its Discontents.* Translated by Joan Riviere (1929) in *Great Books of the Western World.* Edited by Robert M. Hutchins. Chicago: Encyclopedia Britannica, 1952.

Fromm, Erich. *The Anatomy of Human Destructiveness.* New York: Holt, Rinehart, and Winston, 1973.

Gelles, Richard J., and Donileen R. Loseke. *The Violent Home: A Study of Physical Aggression between Husbands and Wives*. Beverly Hills, Calif.: Sage, 1972.

————. *Family Violence*. Beverly Hills, Calif.: Sage, 1979.

Gelles, Richard J., and Donileen R. Loseke, eds. *Current Controversies on Family Violence*. Newbury Park, Calif.: Sage, 1993.

Gibson, James William. *Warrior Dreams: Violence and Manhood in Post-Vietnam America*. New York: Hill and Wang, 1994.

Giles-Sims, Jean. *Wife Battering: A Systems Theory Approach*. New York: Guilford, 1983.

Gilligan, James. *Violence: Reflections on a National Epidemic*. New York: Vintage, 1997.

Girard, René. *Violence and the Sacred*. Translated by Patrick Gregory. Baltimore: Johns Hopkins University Press, 1977.

————. *The Scapegoat*. Translated by Yvonne Freccero. Baltimore: Johns Hopkins University Press, 1986.

Helfer, Mary Edna, Ruth S. Kempe, and Richard D. Krugman, eds. *The Battered Child*. 5th edition, revised and expanded. Chicago: University of Chicago Press, 1997.

Hilton, N. Zoe, ed. *Legal Responses to Wife Assault: Current Trends and Evaluation*. Newbury Park, Calif.: Sage, 1993.

Johnson, Elizabeth A. *She Who Is: The Mystery of God in Feminist Theological Discourse*. New York: Crossroad, 1993.

Jones, Ann. *Next Time, She'll Be Dead: Battering and How to Stop It*. Revised and updated edition. Boston: Beacon, 2000.

Jones, Gregory L. *Embodying Forgiveness: A Theological Analysis*. Grand Rapids, Mich.: Eerdmans, 1995.

Keenan, Dennis King. *Death and Responsibility: The "Work" of Levinas*. Albany: SUNY Press, 1999.

Levinas, Emmanuel. *Totality and Infinity: An Essay in Exteriority*. Translated by Alphonso Lingis. Pittsburgh: Duquesne University Press, 1969.

————. *Ethics and Infinity: Conversations with Philippe Nemo*. Translated by Richard A. Cohen. Pittsburgh: Duquesne University Press, 1985.

Levy, Barrie, ed. *Dating Violence: Young Women in Danger.* Seattle: Seal, 1998.

Lorenz, Konrad. *On Aggression.* Translated by Marjorie Kerr-Wilson. New York: Harcourt, Brace, 1963.

Loseke, Donileen R. *The Battered Woman and Shelters: The Social Construction of Wife Abuse.* Albany: SUNY Press, 1992.

Martos, Joseph. *Doors to the Sacred: A Historical Introduction to Sacraments in the Catholic Church.* Garden City, N.Y.: Doubleday, 1982.

May, Rollo. *Power and Innocence: A Search for the Sources of Violence.* New York: Norton, 1972.

Messner, Michael. *Sex, Violence, and Power in Sports: Rethinking Masculinity.* Freedom, Calif.: Crossing, 1994.

Midgley, Mary. *Beast and Man: The Roots of Human Nature.* Ithaca, N.Y.: Cornell University Press, 1978.

Miedzian, Myriam. *Boys Will Be Boys: Breaking the Link between Masculinity and Violence.* New York: Doubleday, 1991.

Nelson, James B. *The Intimate Connection: Male Sexuality, Masculine Spirituality.* Philadelphia: Westminster, 1988.

Neuger, Christie Cozad, and James Newton Poling, eds. *The Care of Men.* Nashville: Abingdon, 1997.

Parker, Joan C., Barbara Hart, and Jane Stueling. *Seeking Justice: Legal Advocacy Principles and Practice.* Harrisburg: Pennsylvania Coalition Against Domestic Violence, 1992.

Peled, Einat, Peter G. Jaffe, and Jeffrey L. Edleson, eds. *Ending the Cycle of Violence: Community Responses to Children of Battered Women.* Thousand Oaks, Calif.: Sage, 1995.

Pelzer, David. *A Child Called It.* Deerfield Beach, Fla.: Health Communications, 1995.

Pipher, Mary. *Reviving Ophelia: Saving the Selves of Adolescent Girls.* New York: Ballentine, 1994.

Pirog-Good, Maureen A., and Jan E. Stets, eds. *Violence in Dating Relationships.* Westport, Conn.: Praeger, 1989.

Plaskow, Judith, and Carol P. Christ, eds. *Weaving the Visions: New Patterns in Feminist Spirituality.* New York: Harper Collins, 1989.

Prejean, Helen, C.S.J. *Dead Man Walking: An Eyewitness Account of the Death Penalty in the United States.* New York: Vintage, 1993.

Ricoeur, Paul. *The Symbolism of Evil.* Translated by Emerson Buchanon. Boston: Beacon, 1967.

Ruether, Rosemary Radford. *Christianity and the Making of the Modern Family.* Boston: Beacon, 2000.

———. *Sexism and God-Talk: Toward a Feminist Theology.* Boston: Beacon, 1983.

Russell, Diana E. H. *Rape in Marriage.* Bloomington: Indiana University Press, 1982.

Sands, Kathleen M. *Escape from Paradise: Evil and Tragedy in Feminist Theology.* Minneapolis: Fortress Press, 1994.

Schüssler Fiorenza, Elisabeth, and Mary Shawn Copeland, eds. *Violence against Women.* Concilium, vol. 1. Maryknoll, N.Y.: Orbis, 1994.

Schüssler Fiorenza, Francis, and John P. Galvin, eds. *Systematic Theology: Roman Catholic Perspectives.* 2 volumes. Minneapolis: Fortress Press, 1991.

Stanage, Sherman M. *Reason and Violence: Philosophical Investigations.* Totowa, N.J.: Littlefield, Adams, 1974.

Straus, Murray A., Richard J. Gelles, and Suzanne K. Steinmetz. *Behind Closed Doors: Violence in the American Family.* Newbury Park, Calif.: Sage, 1988.

Suchocki, Marjorie Hewitt. *God, Christ, Church: A Practical Guide to Process Theology.* New York: Crossroad, 1988.

———. *The Fall to Violence: Original Sin in Relational Theology.* New York: Continuum, 1995.

Thistlethwaite, Susan Brooks, and Mary Potter Engle, eds. *Lift Every Voice: Constructing Christian Theologies from the Underside.* New York: Harper Collins, 1990.

Tifft, Larry L. *Battering of Women: The Failure of Intervention and the Case for Prevention.* Boulder, Colo.: Westview, 1993.

Tracy, David. *The Analogical Imagination: Christian Theology and the Culture of Pluralism.* New York: Crossroad, 1981.

U.S. Department of Justice, Bureau of Justice Statistics. "Female Victims of Crime," 1991.

van der Dennen, J., and V. Falger, eds. *Sociobiology and Conflict: Evolutionary Perspectives on Competition, Cooperation, Violence, and Warfare*. New York: Chapman and Hall, 1990.

Walker, Lenore E. *The Battered Woman*. New York: Harper and Row, 1979.

————. *The Battered Woman Syndrome*. 2nd edition. New York: Springer, 2000.

Weems, Renita J. *Battered Love: Marriage, Sex, and Violence in the Hebrew Prophets*. Minneapolis: Fortress Press, 1995.

Welch, Sharon D. *A Feminist Ethic of Risk*. Revised edition. Minneapolis: Fortress Press, 2000.

Whitehead, Evelyn E., and James D. Whitehead. *Marrying Well: Stages on the Journey of Christian Marriage*. New York: Doubleday, 1983.

Index